THE OMNIBUS OF PEN SKETCHING

Get, Set & Sketch like a Boss!

HuesAndTones Media and Publishing

THE OMNIBUS OF PEN SKETCHING

Shirish Deshpande

Table of Contents

BOOK 1 - GET-SET-SKETCH!

BOOK 2 - SKETCH LIKE A BOSS!

GET-SET-SKETCH!

Secrets of Pen & Ink Sketching Unleashed!

SHIRISH DESHPANDE

INTRODUCTION

Welcome to "Get-Set-Sketch!", a turbocharged guide to jumpstart your pen and ink sketching experience.

I am glad you made it this far!

The beauty of pen and ink as a medium is that - it is anytime, anywhere! There's no tiresome cleanup afterwards, the materials are (mostly) affordable, and possibilities are endless.

In this book, we will together embark on a magical journey through the realm of inks to create stunning sketches.

So, let's get inking!

Who is this Book for?

Are you a beginner to the art of sketching? Have you been away from sketching for most of your life?

- Are you a passionate artist, who wants to enhance your skills?
- Are you afraid of sketching?
- Are you excited by the mere thought of sketching?
- Are you a hobby artist or a professional?

Then this book is for you! Yes… YOU!

Before We Begin ...

If you are intimidated by sketching, I totally understand you! I have experienced firsthand, how traditional methods and rules of art teaching in schools kill the creativity of students.

Everyone is a born artist. The problem is that most people forget this fact as they grow up.

My mission is to rekindle that creativity and love for art, which every one of us has.

After all, art is THE one quality that separates us from animals.

What do you need to have to learn Sketching?

-Love of art

- An open mind
- An unchained imagination
- Loads of enthusiasm
- Loads of enthusiasm
          and...
- Loads of enthusiasm

The Beginner's Dilemma. What is a good sketch?

Let's start with a basic question. What is a good piece of art?

Let's go to even more basic level. What is art?

Ask this question to a hundred people, and you will get a hundred answers. But one thing is certain - art invokes feelings in us. Those feelings may be happy, sad, erotic, ecstatic, fearful or even grotesque.

Any kind of art form be it auditory, visual or sensory, is a success only when it can invoke feelings in the audience (hopefully the same kind of feelings it's intended to invoke!).

So, let's come back to our original question. What is good art?
Or, to keep us closer to the subject of this book, what is a good sketch?

The most common compliment I get for my sketches/paintings are to the tune of "This looks so real" or better yet, "This looks exactly like a photograph".

And this gem heard recently – "Your sketches are posing a serious competition to the camera!"

SERIOUSLY??

These kinds of comments make me cringe!

Why?

Because though the intentions of these well-wishers are noble, they are unknowingly insulting my sketches!

A sketch is never intended to mimic reality. We have cameras for that!

A sketch is supposed to *enhance* reality. A sketch is a unique expression of the sketcher on a subject.

A photographer has only so much control over what the camera sees and captures. He/she may enhance the photograph later and add/ remove elements as they suit the purpose.

A sketcher has the freedom to choose the elements he/she wants to be part of the sketch at the making stage itself.

A sketcher even has the freedom to sketch only part of a scene and declare the sketch as finished!

See the following two pictures. I have not bothered to complete these and have drawn only selectively. Still, the sketches look complete.

So, all the present and would be sketchers out there… repeat this mantra with me.

I will never try to mimic a photograph.
I will never try to mimic a photograph.
I will never try to mimic a photograph.

See, have you already started feeling better? Isn't that a huge burden off your chest?

Let's make you feel even better.

Have a look at the photograph below, and the sketch based on this photograph. Which one looks better?

See what I mean?

But I couldn't draw a straight line if my life depended on it.

Let me ask you another question. Can you read and write? If you are reading this, I think you can!

Then you can sketch.

Let me elaborate.

Have a look at the following word. What does it say?

"F L O W E R"

Did you just read this word as "flower"? Did you visualize a flower as you read this? Why?

Why did you visualize this word as flower, and not as a rock, or brick, or a pancake?

Because you saw a bunch of lines and circles, which you interpreted as letters, which you in turn used to form a word, and mentally translated it into a very real object.

And every one of us can write this word, right?

"FLOWER"

to

The Omnibus of Pen Sketching

So, every one of us can draw those lines and circles which represent an object. Now all we must do is draw some lines and circles which are visually closer to the reality!

Since this main mental block is out of the way, let's see how we can quickly progress from Abstraction to Reality.

Abstraction vs. Reality

Abstraction is a representation of an object in artistic form.

The extreme form of abstraction, which we use all the time without ever realizing it, is called writing.

Sketching falls somewhere between hyper realism (photograph/photorealistic painting) and total abstraction (writing). The degree to which the sketch will have that abstraction is totally up to you.

But one must follow certain "rules" while deciding this abstraction.

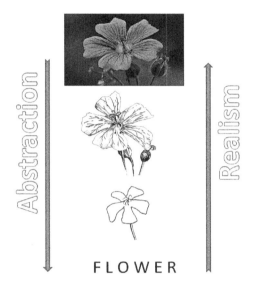

FLOWER

"Rules" of Sketching

Two basic rules govern sketching and art in general.

These are highly authentic, very rigid, and irrefutable rules.

You are not allowed to break or bend these rules under any circumstances!

If you want to be a sketcher, amateur or professional, you must understand and internalize these rules.

Are you ready to unveil these rules?

Let's say it then.

Rule #1 is .. (Drum roll please) that THERE ARE NO RULES!

And Rule #2 is… If you ever start feeling constipated about the "rules" of art, refer to rule #1!

That's it. Now that we have covered the absolute rules of art, let's delve deeper into sketching.

LEARNING TO "SEE"

Have you ever wondered how two people see exactly the same stuff, but one finds it insipid, while the other one finds it inspiring? Have you heard people complaining that they really, really would like to sketch, but don't find any inspiration for sketching? And have you seen someone trying to sketch a lion, but which got sketched out looking like a donkey?

What's the difference between the way an average person sketches and an artist would sketch? Is there such a remarkable difference in skills?

Yes, but not always!

The difference begins with the way both these

If you want to sketch this building, you need to see it differently.

Way 1 – See the shapes
Look at the object as a collection of broad shapes. Do you see rectangles? Polygons? Circles? Squares? Triangles?

Way 2 – See the shadows
Look at the object as a collection of light and shadow shapes.

people "see" things around them.

But I see things all the time, you may say.

Yes, I agree that you see things, but do you really "see" things?

Before you panic, let me explain.

Have a look at this picture. What do you see?

Do you see a building?

If yes, you may not be able to sketch this building!

Why? You may ask.

Because you are not "seeing" the object (building in this case) that you want to sketch the way a sketcher sees it.

There are three ways of "seeing" an object as a sketcher, and we need to learn all three.

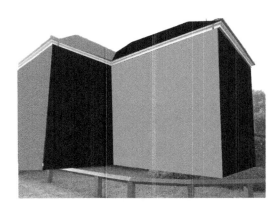

In this picture on the left-hand side, I have marked –
- The darkest shadows as pure black (both the right facing walls),
- Middle tone shadows as grey (middle wall facing us),
- Lightest shadows as very light grey (the leftmost wall).

Way 3 – See the textures

Here I have marked the part of the building with brickwork in black.

Then there's a different texture for various glass windows with their wooden frames.

And the plants partially covering the walls have their own unique texture.

So far, we learned that in order to sketch any object, we need to "see" the following three things:
- Shapes
- Shadows (and light)
- Textures

Now let's learn about some materials we can use for pen and ink sketching.

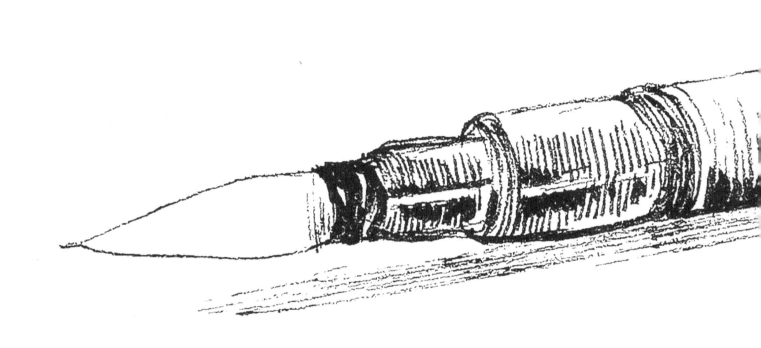

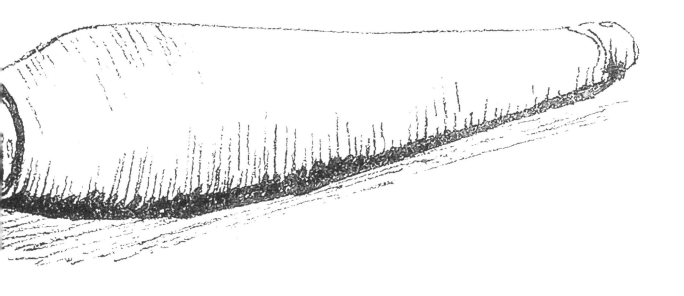

MATERIALS

For basic sketching, you need only two things... a blank paper and a ballpoint pen/gel pen. However, we artists are never satisfied with limited materials. We always want more! So, here's a list of all the materials that I use for pen and ink sketching. This does not mean this is the exhaustive list of materials. The list of materials, just like the list of subjects, is virtually endless. But I will try to provide a starting point for your next shopping list.

Pencil, Eraser and Sharpener

Although entire sketches can be done using a pencil, here I will focus on using a pencil to do rough work for a complete pen and ink sketch.

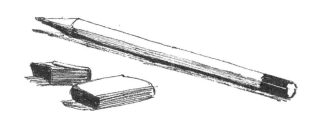

Pencils are of three types:
- "H" type – these are hard pencils which produce very light shades.
- "B" type – very soft pencils which create very dark shades.
- "HB" type – somewhere in between "H" and "B".

Since I use pencils only for rough work in a pen and ink sketch, my intention is to erase these lines later. So, I prefer either "H" or "HB" type pencils.

Is this how I do it? – Yes
Does it have to be done this way? – Refer to Rule #1 at the end of "The Beginner's Dilemma" chapter!

Pens

There are many choices for pens, and each has their own advantages:

Ball point pens/Gel pens – They are very cheap, available in assorted colors and easily available.

When using these pens, make sure you keep a spare rag/rough paper nearby. These pens tend to accumulate ink near their tips, which may result in ugly dots on the sketch.

Make sure you keep wiping the pen tip periodically before, after and during sketching.

I suggest having a white ink ballpoint pen handy as well. These are useful in making corrections, as well as sketching light parts over dark areas.

Technical Pens

These pens are especially made for sketching. They have in-built ink reservoirs. They are available in various tip sizes and I highly recommend them to anyone who is serious about pen & ink sketching.

There are various brands of technical pens available. Some well-known brand names are - Sakura Pigma Micron, Faber-Castell, Brustro, Artliner, Staedtler etc.

You may start with a set of various nib sizes, and then try out various brands as you progress. The feel of each pen may vary, and you would want to test out various brands before settling on one.

These technical pens are available in assorted colors as well.

The Omnibus of Pen Sketching

Here's a sketch done entirely using a ballpoint pen.

Here's a sketch done entirely using technical pens.

Brush Tip Pens

These pens are like technical pens, but they have a brush tip instead of a hard nib. They have in in-built ink reservoir, just like technical pens.

Brush tip pens are especially useful in creating "organic" looking lines. They can also be used to darken large portions of a sketch. More on that later in this chapter.

Brush tip pens are excellent in creating an ink effect without using water.

Brush tip pens are available in assorted colors.

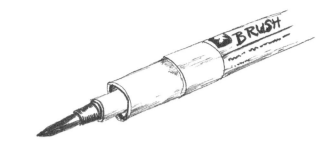

Here's an example of a sketch done mostly using a brush tip pen. The fine fur on the nose and head is sketched using technical pens.

Acrylic Inks:

Inks of various brands and thicknesses are available for sketching. I recommend any ink which is thick and lightfast.

I use inks from two brands, Daler Rowney and Sumi. I have great results with both these. However, you may want to try out different brands before you settle on one or more.

Inks can be applied with watercolor brushes, dip pens, quills, or even twigs! The tools available to apply ink on paper are limited only by your imagination.

These inks are completely waterproof once dry, so they can be applied along with watercolors as well.

Acrylic inks are also available in assorted colors.

Here is an example of inks applied using a dry twig.

Water Brushes:

These brushes have an in-built water reservoir.

These brushes are especially useful when applying thin washes over sketches to depict soft shadows. The reservoir can be squeezed to allow water to flow into the brush tip. The amount of water can be controlled to decide on the amount of ink being dispensed.

Here's an example of a sketch where water brush was used to apply grey shades.

Sketching paper:

The beauty of pen and ink medium is that it can be practiced anywhere.

Even a paper napkin at a restaurant table is enough for a pen sketch.

However, the best results can be obtained by using the right kind of paper for the right kind of sketch.

I will tell you about some of the papers that I have used.

While selecting a paper, you need to consider the following things.
- Paper thickness
- Paper texture

Paper thickness is measured in GSM (Grams per square meter). Without going into details, just understand that the more GSM value is specified for a paper, the thicker it is.

Typical sketchbook papers are available from 50 GSM all the way upwards of 400 GSM thicknesses.

Smaller GSM papers (70-120 GSM) are ok for ball point/technical pen work. But these papers tend to buckle when using water-based inks, or watercolor. Inks and watercolor also tend to seep through these thin papers.

Bigger GSM value papers (upward of 250 GSM) are preferably used for ink and watercolor work.

I typically use 70-120 GSM papers for pen work, and 250-300 GSM Canson/Fabriano papers for inks/watercolor work. I also sometime use Poster Board papers for sketching. They are thick as well as smooth for penwork.

Paper smoothness/roughness can be used to create various textures in the sketch.

Technical pens work better on smooth papers, like Bristol boards or Poster boards.

Watercolor/inks work better on textured/rough papers.

The sketch on the left was done on an ultra-smooth Bristol paper (120 GSM) using only technical pens. Observe the textures created using pen here.

The sketch on the right was done on a semi-textured Canson paper (250 GSM) using technical pens and black India ink. Observe how the paper texture has been used to create a rough stone effect.

Free Resource – Pen and Ink Shading Materials guide

You can download a free Pen and Ink Sketching Materials PDF from the following location:

https://huesandtones.net/materials/

If you subscribe to my newsletter, you will keep getting the updated version of this guide as I try out new materials. You can subscribe using this link:

https://HuesAndTones.net/signup/

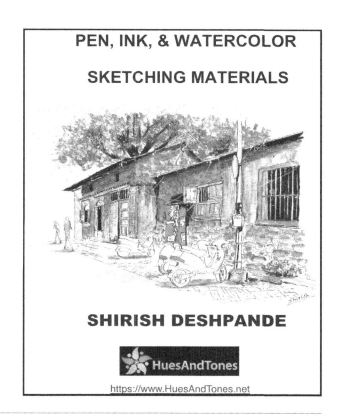

Now go ahead. Do some practice and go on to the next chapter.

Here's an example of hatching being used in the shading:

Shading Technique #2: Cross-hatching

Cross-hatching means doing hatching in more than one direction over one another. That's it. Really! See some examples of cross hatching below, and you will understand.

You can do horizontal hatching and then vertical hatching on top.

Or you can do diagonal hatching.

Or you can combine everything.

Are there any rules? Oh yess. See the end of "The Beginner's Dilemma" chapter for rules!

Now do some practice of cross hatching. Then we will explore the next shading technique.

Here's an example of cross hatching used in shading.

You may use more than one shading technique in the same area. Totally ok. We will see some examples soon.

Do as your gut feeling tell you.

This is art, not a freaking math exam!

Headache for you: Have a look at the sketch on the previous page and see if you can find out all the shading techniques used.

Free Resource – Pen Shading Techniques 'Cheat Sheet'

You can download a free Pen Shading Techniques Cheat Sheet PDF from the following location:

https://HuesAndTones.net/cheatsheet/

This is a quick reference guide to the pen sketching techniques that you have learned so far. You may take a printout of this PDF and use it to practice the pen shading techniques.

USING INK FOR SHADING

Using inks directly to shade sketches is such a big topic that I found it necessary to devote a separate chapter for this one technique.

How should one decide whether to use pens or inks for shading?

To answer that… I will again stress this: This is not a freaking math exam! It's art. You decide by your gut feeling.

And the available materials, of course.

What materials does one require for ink shading?

For starters, an ink bottle. I have suggested a few types of inks in the Materials section. However, you are free to use any brand you are comfortable with.

If you don't know which ink brand you are comfortable with, you need to try out some brands before you settle on one.

Search for "India ink" or "acrylic ink" in the online stores or your local art store.

You will need a few watercolor brushes of various sizes (three-four synthetic brushes are enough), a water brush would be an added advantage.

Keep a small pot containing water handy for washing the brushes. Keep some soft tissue papers handy to wipe the brushes.

I also like to use a toothbrush for adding some interesting effects to the sketch. Here's one example. Look at the interesting effect it has created at the bottom of the hut.

Of course, the materials that you can use have no limits. You may use twigs, toothpicks, tissue papers, plastic sheets, tooth brushes, fingers, or any other tools you may think of.

You may use a brush tipped pen to create the same effect as a brush creating a dark shade.

Both pens and inks have their own beauty. So one cannot really say that one of them is better than the other.

But when it comes to shading large areas, using inks decidedly reduces one's efforts.

Inks, along with brushes and other tools, creates more "organic" lines, while pens create more uniform lines.

Again, one is not better than the other. You may use both in combination as well for their advantages.

You can either use ink to create very dark shades, or grey tones. Both these methods have their own advantages. One is not necessarily better than the other.

The Omnibus of Pen Sketching

Whether to use pens, inks with dark shades, or inks with grey tones, or a combination of these, is totally up to your gut feeling and the materials available.

These are how the various strokes look.

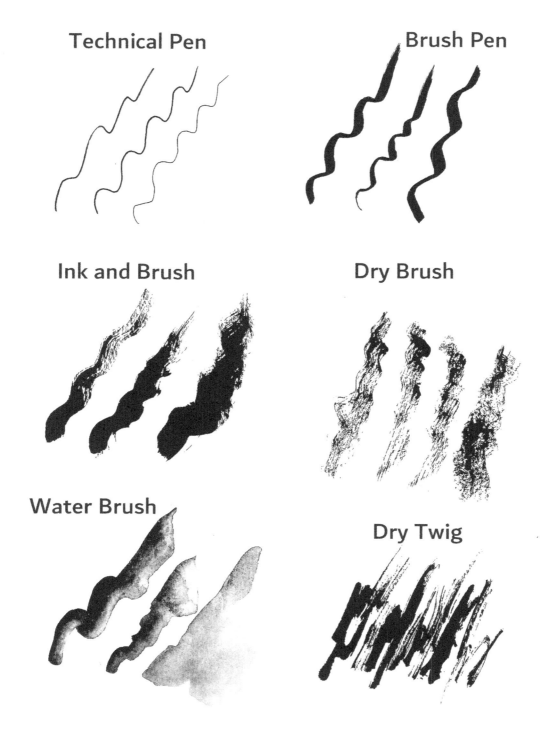

Technical Pen

Brush Pen

Ink and Brush

Dry Brush

Water Brush

Dry Twig

Now let's learn in detail how to sketch various objects using pen and inks. We will cover various topics and learn about specific shading methods used for creating textures. Let's start with a topic where there's very low probability to go wrong!

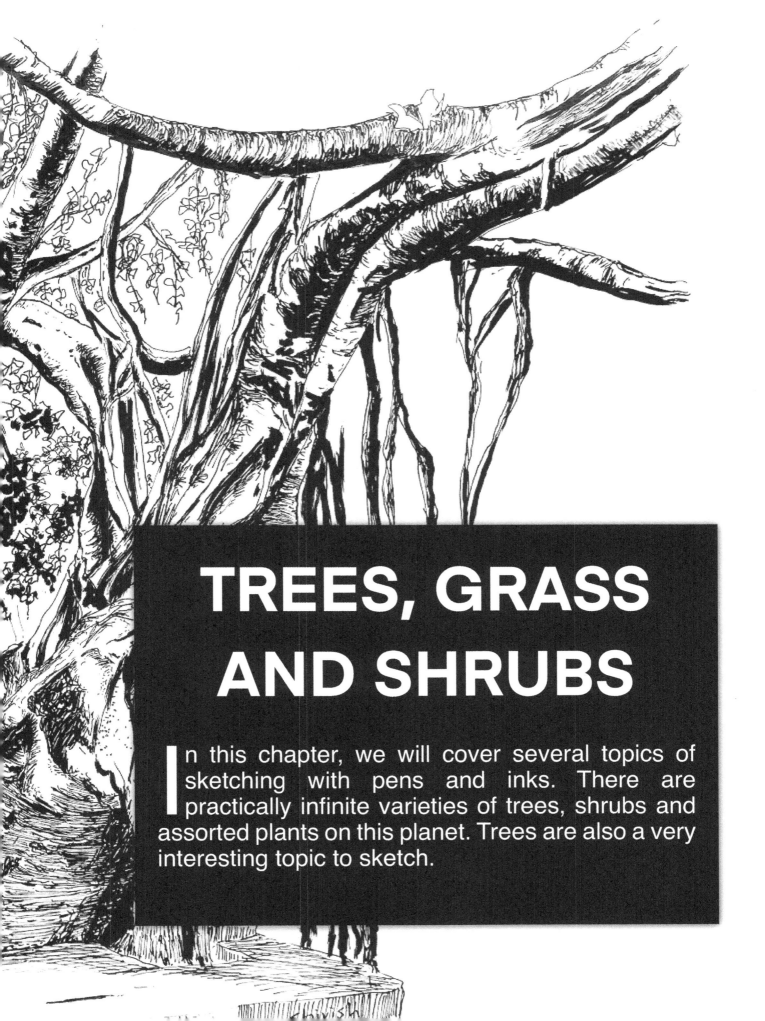

TREES, GRASS AND SHRUBS

In this chapter, we will cover several topics of sketching with pens and inks. There are practically infinite varieties of trees, shrubs and assorted plants on this planet. Trees are also a very interesting topic to sketch.

Tree and shrub leaves pose an interesting challenge to sketch, because sketching every leaf is not practical, and sketching just the outline is not enough!

Tree barks present interesting challenges (and opportunities) to experiment with various textures.

Below, I have shown tree bark (from left) in exquisite details and with somewhat less details.

Here's a tree shown completely silhouetted.

Note that there are gaps between leaves. These are called "sky holes" and they should be left out in leaves to make the sketch more believable.

Never fill up the entire area of the tree canopy.

The Omnibus of Pen Sketching

How much detail you want to put into your sketch depends on the topic at hand, sketch composition, time at hand, and of course, the artist's mood.

Artist's mood? Is such a thing even important? Hell yeah!

But anyway, speaking of trees...

The best way to practice sketching trees is to observe the plant life around you and sketch it.

Remember to use the contour method of shading to emphasize textures. The tree trunks are typically cylindrical in shape, and the curve of the bark must be emphasized while drawing texture.

Below, I have shown a few examples of tree trunks. Of course, just like anything in nature, the varieties are endless.

See how a few simple contour strokes, combined with light and dark areas, pop out the volume and rough texture of the bark.

This is a quick sketch of the trunk of a (date) palm tree. See how the interlocking parts of the bark are indicated with few dark strokes.

When sketching trees, focus on the overall effect, not on too many details.

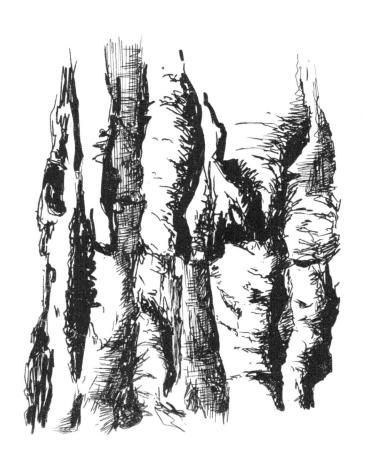

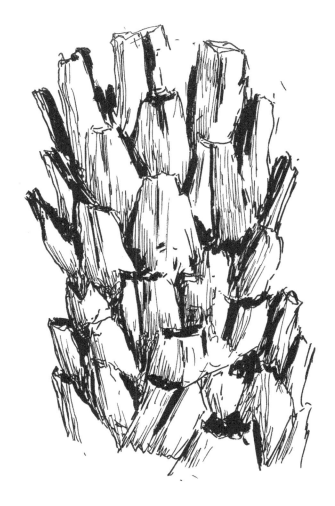

Trees are often juxtaposed against grass/other trees or other objects. Here, the two trunks on the foreground, along with some grass, act as the main subjects of interest.

To highlight them, and push everything else in the background, I have used vertical hatching strokes.

Vertical hatching strokes are super useful when sketching out-of-focus backgrounds. I have used the same kind of strokes in the "headache" exercise I gave you at the end of "Shading Techniques" chapter.

There was too much visual clutter in this image. There's a background chain link fence, and two bamboo sticks in the foreground, along with a slew of plants.

To get better visual clarity, I have selectively used dark shades, and kept details of leaves in some areas to a minimum. Also, I took special care to make sure lines in the background fence were relatively straight. Rarely are lines so straight in nature, and that creates a stark contrast between this artificial object and natural plants.

This is part of a sketch where the contour lines for bark texture are juxtaposed against the random strokes for leaves.

Observe again how the contrast between various shading techniques helps in visual clarity to a sketch which would otherwise have been very cluttered.

Also see how white spaces are important in bringing about the visual clarity.

Without white spaces, this sketch would be a jumble on unrecognizable pen strokes.

White spaces are as important as pen/ink work in a sketch.

STONES AND ROCKS

Stones and rocks are another "safe" subject to draw, which means you don't need as much accuracy as say portraits or buildings. However, we need to be much more aware of values when sketching rocks.

Rocks are of different types like hard rocks, rocks with sharp edges, smooth pebbles, grainy rocks etc.

Just like trees and shrubs, there are practically infinite varieties of rocks.

We will see how to sketch a few of these varieties.

Rock with hard edges - This is a fun type of rock to draw, since there are so many opportunities to draw hard edges and dark spaces in the nooks and crevices.

Note the fine lines drawn on the surface of rocks. It's important not to overdo drawing these to avoid clutter.

Here's another example of rough rocks with some moss on them.

Notice how the moss is represented using stippling.

Big rocks in arid regions - These are intentionally shaded very dark in the shadow region so that the white part appears brighter.

These rocks have comparatively smoother surfaces but have a lot of cracks and nooks.

Notice the minimal detailing, and mostly dark values in the shadow region.

Smooth pebbles - The smoothness is emphasized by minimal shading.

However, the rocks are not entirely "glass smooth". They have fine freckle-like patterns on them. These patterns are shown using stippling. The rougher patches on the rocks are shown using hatching/cross hatching.

Stones and Rocks

ANIMAL FUR

While sketching animal fur, we use a type of stroke which is a variant of hatching. This type of stroke is called "criss-cross hatching". This hatching is like what we use for the grass.

While using criss-cross hatching to sketch animal fur, remember these two important points:

- Animal fur radiates out from animal bodies/ faces.
- There's no one uniform patch of fur on an animal. Instead, there are various clumps of fur.

In this Panda sketch, observe how the fur on the face appears to be radiating towards the extremities of the face.

Also note how much space is kept empty! It's never too much to emphasize that white spaces are as important as the ink itself.

The Omnibus of Pen Sketching

In this lion sketch below, see how the criss-cross pen strokes radiate outward to indicate the mane.

The cross-hatching strokes drawn with the same pen, however, indicate non-hairy areas on the face.

One can use the brush + pens combination to depict fur as well, as shown in these two examples.

Here, I have used light grey shades, followed by fine criss-cross lines.

WOOD

Wood, as used in the construction of houses, barns and doors, is an interesting subject to sketch.

Shading for bringing out the texture in wood is easy. I will show it below.

However, the sketch will really come out well when one understands the character of the place beyond the simple looking wood.

Have a look at this wooden door and tell me if you don't just see the wood, but also decades of human memories and emotions attached to this door!

This is not just a door, it's a story of the place!

I am getting emotional here!

Give me a couple of minutes and I will be back (sob).

So... where was I?

Ahh, I was going to tell you how to draw the wood texture.

Right!

So here's the secret. Ready?

Look at this picture of a few wooden planks side by side.

You can notice 2 types of strokes here:

1. Those running vertically along the length of the wood. These are vertical and broken. Also notice that even though they are parallel to each other, no two adjacent strokes are the same in length.

The strokes are also slightly wavy, rather than straight.

2. Those which are semi-circular, are having the legacy of the tree from which the wood is extracted. Again notice how the strokes are left kinda halfway.

Apart from these, there are some small holes in the wood. Together these factors provide a natural feel to the wood sketch.

Because the gaps between planks are vertical, and the strokes on the planks are also vertical, how do we visually separate the planks?

They are separated from each other by thickening the gaps between planks. Here we are using dark values to indicate separation between planks and light values for the texture on the planks themselves.

On top of the texture lines are thin strokes to indicate shadows.

The Omnibus of Pen Sketching

One important thing to always keep in mind… Never give in to the temptation of doing "some more texturing". See the picture below for the example of how to draw minimum texture on the wood.

Waterfall

Waterfalls have bubbling, white water.

When sketching a waterfall using pen and inks, give more emphasis on the area surrounding the waterfall, rather than the waterfall itself.

Some strategically placed lines within the main body of the waterfall are enough to indicate the rushing water.

Just like sketching any other water body, it's important not to go overboard with drawing these lines, though.

River

River water is not as calm as a lake, but it's calmer than a waterfall.

The shape of the river is what defines it, and its shape can be depicted using its surroundings.

Here the river is shown to be winding its way through the landscape. Notice how the details of the landscape keep getting less and less in the picture. This provides the feel of distance.

Seashore

Seashore can be rocky or flat. For rocky seashore, waves keep crashing into the rocks, creating dramatic splashes. When sketching such splashes, we can use stippling to great effect to create the "spray" effect.

On a calm seashore, a patch of wet sand forms where the waves keep advancing and retreating over the land.

This patch of wet, packed sand can be used to sketch interesting reflections.

SHADING TECHNIQUES EXERCISES

Let's draw these two illustrations. We will learn to draw the first illustration (Palm Trees near a Pond) using pens only. Then we will learn to draw the second illustration (The House in a Ghost Town) using pens and ink.

Pen Sketching Exercise – Palm Trees near a Pond

Now let's use the following reference photograph to do a complete sketch using the techniques we learned.

You may download the reference photographs, final images and the linework for both demos from the following URL (or scan the QR code on the right):

https://HuesAndTones.net/gssreferences/

Before we begin, keep this in mind.

What I am showing you is a guideline. You may follow it for understanding. But this is not the only right way to do sketching.

You may do any kind of variations to the techniques I show you, and you will still be right.

You don't need to exactly copy the photograph. You may take any liberty related to composition, lighting, textures, or anything for that matter.

As I have already said earlier, "This is art, not a freaking Math test!".

Let's begin by dividing the reference photograph into a 3 X 3 grid.

To understand why we do this, we will digress a bit and discuss something called "Rule of Thirds".

Whaaat? There's a rule for sketching? But I had just said a few chapters ago that there are only two rules to sketching? Where did this third rule come from?

Hold your guns, people. It's named as "Rule", but it's only a "rule of thumb".

This "rule" applies to compositions of all kind of visual arts like sketching, painting, photography and even filmmaking, and it's very simple.

A composition looks more pleasant when the main subjects are kept away from the center.

When we click a picture, or sketch a picture, the first impulse is to keep all the interesting things bang in the middle. Avoid this impulse.

Keeping the main subject away from the center creates a slight imbalance in the composition, which draws the viewer's interest.

Do you see the rule of thirds applied in this photograph?

You don't need to do exact division like this, just be aware of it mentally.

You may draw the same grid on the paper where you will be doing the final sketch.

Don't use a ruler to draw this grid! And keep the lines very loose and faint. We will be erasing them later.

Also keep some space marked away from all corners of the paper. You don't want to spill over the paper.

As you may have noticed, most of the sketches that I have included in this book do not have well-defined borders.

Forget what they taught you in school. A sketch neither needs to have a fixed border, nor is it necessary for it to fill the entire sheet of paper.

As I keep repeating throughout this book… White spaces are as important as black lines.

Hmm, now that I am done doling out philosophy, I will make myself useful and actually do what I am supposed to do, that is, tell you how to proceed with the sketch.

We will start with a rough pencil sketch. This sketch is not meant to be very detailed.

The pencil sketch is meant to block in the larger shapes, so we can limit the scope of our sketch.

Here's the outline of the pencil sketch I made prior to pen work.

The lines are sketched thick only for your understanding. In reality, the pencil lines should be so light that they should be visible only to you.

You may observe that in addition to marking the broad shapes, I have marked dark values (with complete blacks / horizontal lines).

Right now, the focus is not on accuracy, but to get the shapes and shadows right.

Remember the chapter "Learning to see"? We are blocking two out of the three elements we discussed in that chapter (shapes and shadows).

We will worry about textures when we do pen work.

Now that the rough sketch is ready, let's look at finishing this sketch using pen work.

For this exercise, I will use technical pens. You are free to use technical pens, or ballpoint/gel pen.

The advantage of technical pens is the freedom to sketch using various tip sizes. But they are not an absolute must. Keep a white inked ballpoint pen handy for finishing touches. This is optional. Let's start with pen work.

When doing pen and ink work, it's prudent to start with shapes which are closest to us, as these shapes will overlap others.

I started with this bunch of large leaves in the foreground. As of now, they are not very "polished". But they provide some semblance to the leaves. That's enough for now.

These leaves are drawn with a medium thick (0.3) tip pen.

Now we will draw the outline for trees. Since light is falling on the trees from the right side, we will make the left side of the trees slightly darker.

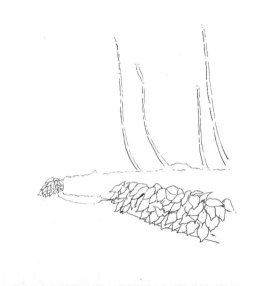

For the left side of the trees, I will be using a 0.3 thick tip pen, while for the right side; I will use 0.1 tip pen. Also note that I have kept the lines randomly broken at places. We can always complete them later. No need to be too precise as of now.

The Omnibus of Pen Sketching

Also note that the trees are slightly "floating" above the ground! This is because we are going to cover the base of trees with some grass, and we need to keep this space empty.

Notice that the lower edge of the shore is drawn holding the clump of leaves we sketched earlier. See how the leaves are overlapping the edge.

Now we will draw the mysterious mini-pillars behind the clump of leaves on the lower right side.

Points to note for drawing these pillars:

The pillars appear to float in the air, as their lower ends will be covered in grass.

For each pillar, some area on the top is marked. This is where the light will fall, creating highlights. We will not make this area dark like rest of the pillar.

Some stones in the water are also sketched. Keep the lower edge of each stone flat, regardless of the overall stone shape.

Sketch the grass and some foliage at the far end of the little piece of land.

Notice how the grass is drawn with minimum criss-cross strokes. It's important not to overdo sketching grass. Since the grass is at the far end, its details should be less visible.

The foliage is sketched using random strokes and a thin (0.1) tip pen. Same for grass.

The mini pillars are now completely darkened, except those areas marked for highlights.

Next, we mark the stokes of the palm fronds. Note how the fronds radiate outward from the tree. Stokes ("Spines" of the fronds) of the closer tree are marked thicker.

Now we will complete the details of the palm fronds.

For the fronds directly facing us, we need to sketch the pinnae (leaves) on both sides of the stock. For the fronds facing away, we need to sketch the pinnae on only one side.

There will be a massive, mind-numbing overlap between the fronds. It's ok. One does not need to be too accurate as of now. We can cover up every error later using shading.

Now we will add some texture to the tree trunks. For this, do these two things:

1. Make the left edges of the trees (away from light), very dark with thick pen. Here, I have used a 0.4 tip pen to darken the tree edges.
2. Using horizontal contour strokes, intermittently sketch over the tree trunk. Don't sketch too many strokes. We just need to give a feel of the texture.

Sketch the texture most prominently on the closest of the trees. Do this using a thin tipped pen.

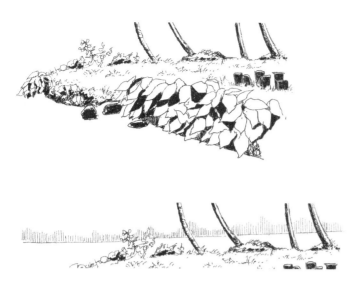

Add some dark shadows to the leaves near the shore.

Now draw a horizontal line indicating the horizon as shown here. This line should be drawn with a thin tip pen, because we are indicating a long distance here.

Draw the faint outline of hills and shrubs over this line using HB pencil. Then carefully draw vertical hatching strokes from horizon line to the pencil line as shown here.

For these hatching strokes, use the thinnest tip pen you have at your disposal.

Erase the pencil line after the strokes are completed.

Let's add some reflections in the water.

The reflections nearer to the shore will be very dark. As we move away from the shore, they become gradually lighter (and broken with some white spaces).

Keep some white spaces to indicate breaks in the shadows as shown here.

Some horizontal pen strokes here and there are enough to indicate calm water.

Now our sketch looks like this.

Now it's time to add some finishing touches. I am using a very thin tip pen (Pigma micron 0.005) and a white Uniball ball point pen for finishing touches.

It totally depends on you when you deem your sketch complete. For me, the most difficult part is to decide when a sketch is complete!

One hint - when you feel the sketch is complete, stop right there and get over the urge to overdo it.

Easier said than done, I know!

The completed sketch (for me!) is shown on the next page.

Don't forget to sign it! You have earned it :-)

Pen and Ink Sketching Exercise – The House in a Ghost Town

Let's use the following reference photograph to draw the above sketch using pen and ink. (Original photograph by Yann Allegre from Unsplash).

One thing to note: I have not included all the elements in the reference photograph in the final sketch. The hanging wire at the top, the excess foliage at the bottom, and the surrounding hills are all missing from the final sketch.

When drawing a sketch, it's your choice what you want to include and what you want to leave out. There's nothing right or wrong about it.

In the following picture, the original photograph is divided using a 3X3 grid.

This has nothing to do with the rule of thirds.

The main subject of this picture, aka the house, is stark in the middle of the frame. So, the rule of thirds does not apply here.

The grid is just for our understanding of the placement of various elements in the picture. You may skip this step if you are comfortable with drawing it freehand.

The picture on the left shows the initial outline sketch. You do not need to be super-accurate at this stage. First draw a rough sketch using a light pencil. I normally use an HB pencil for the rough sketches.

While drawing the pencil sketch, keep the strokes light so they can be easily erased after the penwork is finished.

You may take a printout of the reference sketch provided at the URL mentioned in the beginning of this chapter, and trace over it to draw the initial sketch.

You may notice that the lines in this drawing are not perfectly straight. That's because I drew them without using a ruler.

Having the lines not perfectly straight is however an advantage in a sketch! These lines feel more organic and attractive than the perfectly straight lines.

Note that the bottom part of the house is left empty. We will fill it up by the overlapping foliage later in the drawing process.

Add dark shades to the sketch as shown below. I have used a fountain pen filled with waterproof black ink to fill in these dark areas.

You may achieve the same result by applying acrylic black ink using a watercolor brush or using a black brush pen.

Some points to note:

Observe the shading underneath the slanting roofs of the left-hand and right-hand sides. See how some white gaps are left out in the dark undersides of these roofs.

Do not make these undersides completely dark. A small amount of light will always reflect from the protruding objects like the supporting wooden beams under these roofs.

If you paint these spaces completely black, they will look less like shadows and more like black holes!

Also note how I have kept the white space for the edges of these windowpanes in the shadow. This is not exactly technically correct. But as a sketcher, we can (and should) take such liberties. Our goal is to make the sketch interesting and understandable to the viewer, not photorealistic.

Let's add some textures. Observe how some parallel lines on the planks create the wood-like texture. Refer the techniques from the chapter 'Trees, Grass and Shrubs' to draw such wooden textures.

Leaving some white spaces in the dark shadows also creates a sense of texture as shown in the picture below. Observe the area between both sides of the door and the windows.

This is how the sketch looks after adding textures.

Draw some foliage covering the front side of the house. Mostly, this foliage is tall grass. Draw vertical strokes using pen to show these grass blades.

This is wild grass, not manicured garden. So, the strokes should be random and free. There's zero possibility of going wrong here.

Just make sure you do not obscure too many details of the house while drawing these grass blades.

Add some texture to the machine in the front-right hand side (I am not sure what is the purpose of this machine. So, let's refer to it simply as 'the machine'). Add texture using some randomly spaced vertical strokes as shown below.

There's no need to add details to this machine. We do not want to bring the machine into sharp focus. The focus should always be on the main subject, aka the house.

Draw some grass blades overlapping the machine.

This is how the sketch looks like now.

We will begin the inking process now to add grey shades. You may use a dark black ink in the diluted form or use a grey/not-so-dark ink/ black watercolor to paint grey shades.

I have used Liquitex acrylic ink (Carbon Black) to shade the sketch. In my experience, this ink is not as dark as the Sumi acrylic ink that I normally use. So, I use it like a grey ink. If you do not have access to such light shade, you may simply use a dark ink/watercolor by diluting it with water.

For adding the grey tones and corresponding textures, I dip the damp brush in the ink. Then I get rid of excess ink by rubbing the brush against the edge of the ink bottle.

When I am satisfied with the quantity of paint remaining in the brush, I gently paint the brushstrokes, following the direction of the object being painted.

If you use a dark ink, make the brush wet with water. Then lightly touch the brush to the surface of the ink in the bottle. Let the brush soak in the ink. Wet the brush again with more water. Rub it lightly against a tissue paper/rag to get rid of the excess water. Then use it to

shade.

It's always better to practice the brushstrokes on a rough piece of paper before you shade the main sketch. This practice piece should have the same texture as the paper on which you are drawing the sketch.

Let's see how the brush strokes are applied to the various places.

On the planks, the brush strokes are painted from top to the bottom, leaving plenty of white spaces. Since the brush was not very wet while painting, the brushstrokes appear broken. This resulted in adding more texture to the planks.

The glass panes of these windows are dirty and full of dust. So, they are not as clear and reflective as a clean glass. But they do have a little luster to them. To indicate this luster, I have left some white space on these windowpanes. Since the glass is smooth, there are no other texture marks on them.

For painting the machine, just add strokes from top to bottom and leave plenty of white spaces. Keep the shading minimal.

This is how the house will look after adding the grey tones.

Paint dark shadows using ink in the foliage. Use grey tones to paint some background foliage. Take special care to paint in between the wooden pillars. This will create a sense of depth. If there's nothing but empty space between he pillars, the viewer may even think that that space is another wall!

Use a white ballpoint pen/gel pen to draw grass blades where they overlap with the dark background. This will visually separate them from the background.

Add any finishing touches you desire, and the sketch is complete!

The Omnibus of Pen Sketching

Ready for Some Color?

If you would like to continue your sketching journey into the realm of colors, 'Pen, Ink and Watercolor Sketching - Learn to Draw and Paint Stunning Illustrations in 10 Step-by-Step Exercises' is the perfect next step for you. The unpredictability of the watercolor has always been the main hurdle in using it for many people. We will learn to harness this unpredictability, celebrate the happy accidents, and combine the watercolor with pen and ink to create stunning illustrations.

Check out these books here.

https://HuesAndTones.net/books/

Ready for Some Perspective?

Composition and perspective are vital factors when drawing realistic sketches. They are like the spices and salt in an exotic dish. No one notices them as separate ingredients in the dish. But everyone knows when they are absent!

However, the main problem with most of the perspective books is that they are too technical and focus on architectural perspective. Focusing too much on technical stuff makes one lose the spontaneity in a sketch, which is the soul of the sketch.

So, I devised my own method to draw with an accurate perspective while still keeping the liveliness of the sketch intact.

I share all my composition and perspective secrets for drawing beautiful, expressive sketches in my (very imaginatively titled) 'Composition and Perspective'.

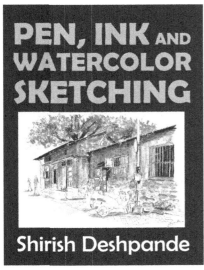

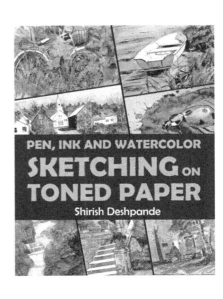

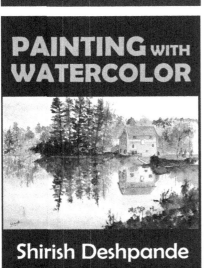

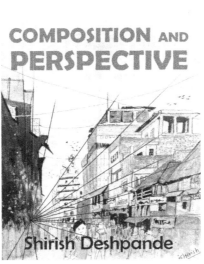

FREE VIDEO TRAINING AND INSPIRATION

You can watch me apply the pen and ink shading techniques I have discussed in this book in the free training courses below.

If you find my sketching speed too slow, you can speed up the videos to a pace that you are most comfortable with.

Both the courses are more than 1.5 hours in length each. In these courses you will learn to apply the pen shading techniques (in Twin Trees) and pen/ink shading techniques (in Temple Street).

The Twin Trees – Pen Shading Techniques

Click the following link (or use the QR code) to watch:

https://www.huesandtones.net/twintrees/

The Temple Street – Pen and Ink Shading Techniques

Click the following link (or use the QR code) to watch:

https://www.huesandtones.net/templestreet/

Inspiration

Gratitude

I am extremely grateful to my wife Aparna, who has consistently stood with me, encouraged me and tolerated me through all my art endeavors and eccentricities.

I am thankful to the following fellow artists, authors and creatives, who reviewed the book manuscript very patiently and came up with suggestions which catapulted the quality of this book by quantum leaps. You guys are incredible.

- Sanjeev Joshi
- Preetam Tiwari
- Shamika Nair
- Deepak Satarkar

Happy Sketching :-)

Dear Reader

'Get-Set-Sketch' kickstarted my journey as an author in August of 2019. The material for this book was being developed over some years, and it had already manifested in the form of some online courses and live training.

I had never expected the overwhelmingly positive response Get-Set-Sketch got. But life (especially that of an author) is full of ups and downs. Most of these ups and downs appear in the form of reviews. And just as challenges in life are our greatest teachers, negative reviews teach us the most, if we care to listen.

One especially negative review for Get-Set-Sketch had mentioned the following:
'I don't think it would help greatly somebody new to sketching. The coverage of important points of sketching is perfunctory. A more experienced sketcher won't find much here.'.

However, it was the last sentence of the review that got my attention:

'The final chapter that walks you through various steps of a drawing is the best part of the book.'.

This line proved to be the key inspiration for 'Sketch like a Boss!'. A book which teaches the reader to draw using exquisitely detailed step-by-step demonstrations are rare, and I thought such a book would really help someone enthusiastic enough to learn.

Since 'Sketch like a Boss' is a natural successor to 'Get-Set-Sketch', it was the logical next step to club them together in a box set.

And here they are. I am sure these two books together will keep you busy and happy for a long time with their rich content.

Read on to 'Sketch like a Boss!'.

Don't forget to subscribe to my newsletter using this link. You get a free downloadable PDF copy of my Adult Coloring Book 'Dystopian Encounters – Wave 1' + a handy reference PDF containing information about the various materials used for pen and ink sketching + periodic tips and tricks for sketching, notifications about my free training videos and much more.

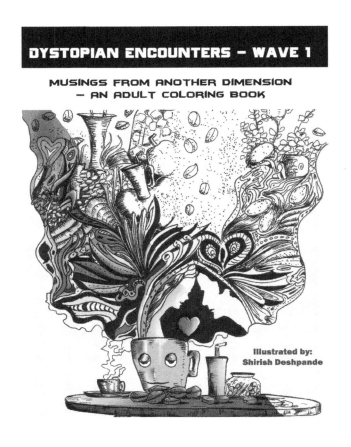

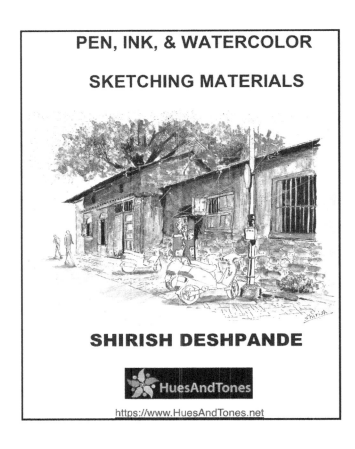

All you need to do is go to the following link and enter your email ID in the box provided.

https://huesandtones.net/signup/

Continue reading 'Sketch like a Boss!'

SKETCH
LIKE A BOSS!

From Novice to a Boss Illustrator in Twenty Easy Steps

SHIRISH DESHPANDE

INTRODUCTION

Who Is This Book For?

The focus of this book is on pen drawing.

Are you interested in learning pen drawing hands-on, from simple to complex subjects? Then this book is for you.

Have you sketched using ballpoint pens/gel pens/technical pens before and want to explore further possibilities? Then this book is for you.

Have you never drawn using pens before and would like to learn this wonderful medium? Then this book is for you.

Do you draw in other mediums, and find pen drawing to be a daunting and unforgiving medium?

Then this book is definitely for you.

What Is This Book About?

Pen drawing is a unique art form. It's super convenient, requires minimum materials (at least for starting up) and is anytime-anywhere.

One doesn't need to prepare a lot before starting a pen illustration. A paper and a pen are enough to start. One doesn't need a lot of space for doing a pen illustration, and there's no or minimum cleanup after the illustration is done.

This book will hold your hand (metaphorically, of course) and guide you through the process of drawing.

The book is arranged into four parts.

The part about the materials required and basic shading techniques is already covered in 'Get-Set-Sketch' and is omitted from this part of the omnibus to avoid repetition.

You can download (for free) a handy PDF of Materials for Pen and Ink Drawing from here:

https://HuesAndTones.net/materials/

Part 1 will introduce you to the concepts of light and shadows, as well as textures. We will deal with only monochrome illustrations in this book. So, understanding shadows is especially important. We do not have the assistance of colors to differentiate between various objects and have only the tool of contrast at our disposal to do so.

Depicting textures is where the true power of pen illustrations comes into play. After learning to create textures, I promise you will never look at the world around you in the same way you do now! We will learn to create textures in the actual demonstrations. But in Part 1, I will show you some hacks that I frequently employ to quickly bring about textures. We will also look at two basic perspective concepts and some hacks to insert human figures quickly into our landscape sketches.

Parts 2, 3, and 4 will guide you in drawing various types of illustrations using pens, step-by-step. We will start with simple illustrations, and gently move towards more complex subjects.

Repetition of Instructions

Within Parts 2 to 4, you will find many pen drawing demonstrations. While reading these demonstrations, you are bound to feel that some of the instructions are repeated. This is by design.

The book is designed with readers of all skill levels in mind. I totally understand that if you find an exercise too trivial for your skill level, you may want to directly jump to a more challenging exercise. Alternatively, you may want to start with a subject which interests you the most.

To allow this free 'jumping around' for the readers, I have repeated several instructions in all the exercises. This will make sure that you can enjoy each demonstration as a stand-alone exercise.

The final illustrations, rough drawings and original reference photographs (if any) are shared on the following web page. Feel free to download these references and use the rough drawings to trace over while starting out with the illustrations.

https://HuesAndTones.net/slabreferences/

The Fear of Making Mistakes

When I ask my students what is the #1 reason why they hesitate to start pen drawing, do you know what they answer?

It's the fear of making mistakes.

Almost everyone starting out with pen drawing is of the opinion that correcting any mistakes is impossible.

Nothing can be further from the truth!

When you see a finished pen illustration like this…

…it's only natural to think that every pen stroke in the illustration was drawn with a sure hand, and any mistake would have instantly ruined the illustration.

But you will be glad to know, that the above illustration started like this:

If you look carefully, you will notice that the church door is drawn a bit crooked, and the left edge of the church door is almost embedded inside the ground!

But these mistakes are completely covered up in the final illustration.

No artist, however accomplished, can draw without making any mistakes.

In fact, mistakes make an artist… The Artist!

I am not ashamed to admit that I commit many mistakes while drawing all the time. And you will too.

But the most important thing is to not let these mistakes bog us down.

That's why I proudly showcase all the mistakes I have made while drawing these illustrations within the demonstrations.

The goal of writing this book is not to impress you with my illustration skills. The goal is to instill confidence in you that you will be able to draw… *like a boss!*

Some 'Ground Rules' While Reading This Book

Throughout this book, we will learn to draw various subjects through step-by-step demonstrations. While you may wish to start imitating the way I do my illustrations, you must keep in mind that the ways I show you are not the only correct ways.

There's only one rule for creating art.

The Rule is that there are no rules!

Every artist starts his/her journey by copying other artists, and so shall you. But after getting the hang of the tools and techniques, you should try different ways of doing things and carve your own path.

In this book, I will show you different ways of drawing using pens. But I do not claim that these methods are the only correct ones or the best ones.

This is the same reason you will rarely find me mentioning the tip size of a pen while illustrating a stroke.

I will provide general guidelines, but I want you to draw using your gut feel and intuition, rather than me spoon-feeding you.

In art, there are multiple 'right' ways of doing things. So, experiment a lot, make many mistakes, and you are sure to grow as an artist.

The Focus Area of This Book

The focus of this book is drawing expressive illustrations, rather than architecturally accurate illustrations.

Now I will explain that sentence in plain language!

It means we will strive to draw beautiful and visually appealing illustrations. However, we will not get too constipated about getting all the measurements right.

For this same reason, we will not ever use a measuring scale for drawing any of our illustrations.

Of course, we will not use 'being expressive' as an excuse for being sloppy! Our illustrations will still look realistic and believable, but the focus will be on beauty and spontaneity.

I am sure by the time you have finished with the exercises in this book, you will be confident enough to draw some cool stuff using pens.

PART 1:
SHADOWS,
TEXTURE HACKS,
HUMAN FIGURES
AND
PERSPECTIVE

Shadows (and Highlights)

Form shadow - This shadow is formed over the object in that area which is facing away from the light. Form shadow becomes darker as we move away from the light source.

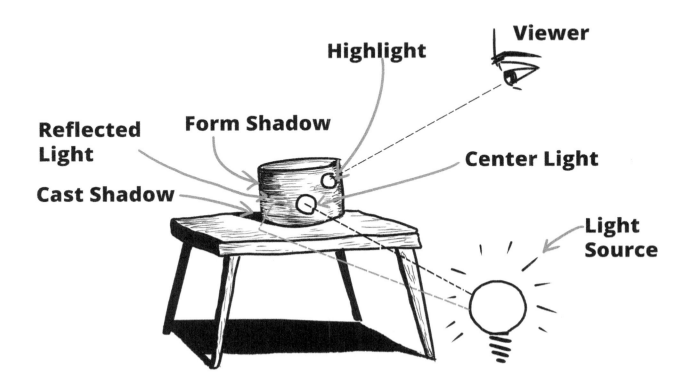

Cast Shadow - This shadow is cast by the object onto the surface over which the object is resting. A cast shadow is the darkest where it attaches to the object and progressively becomes lighter as it moves away from the object.

Reflected Light - Some light may bounce back from the resting surface on to the area with the form shadow. This makes the form shadow lighter.

Center Light - Center light is the area over the object where the incident light is the brightest. Typically, this area is directly in front of the light source. Regardless of where the viewer is observing the object, the center light remains the same (as long as the light source and target object remain stationary).

Highlight - Highlight is the area where the light seems to hit the objects directly to the viewer. If the viewer moves, the highlight moves.

Textures Hacks

Let's see some hacks to draw textures using pens. We will use all these textures in Parts 2 through 4 within various demonstrations in this book. So, paying attention now will save a lot of effort for you later.

But before going ahead, here's one disclaimer.

You will see this disclaimer in many places throughout this book.

Ready? Here it comes…

The hacks and techniques that I show you here (or anywhere in this book) are meant to enable you to make a quick start with pen drawing. I have used many of these techniques successfully and I can vouch for them.

But they are not the only correct ways of drawing with pens!

Art, by its very nature, is fluid. You may create an artwork using five different methods, and each of these may be correct.

And yet, someone may invent a sixth, seventh, or tenth method of creating the same artwork, and all these methods would be correct.

The gist of the story – There is no one right way to do something in art. That's why I will urge you to treat this book as a guideline rather than truth set in stone.

Do copy my techniques but use your intuition and imagination as well. Experiment with different techniques, and you will eventually find your calling.

I wish you very happy sketching!

Let's begin with the hacks.

Wood

The easiest and the fastest way to draw wood texture is using 'dashes and dots'.

In the following picture, I have shown five wooden planks side-by-side. See how drawing a few dashes and dots in a certain pattern automatically lends it a wooden texture.

We need to differentiate between the lines drawn for texture and the lines drawn to indicate the gaps between the planks. This is achieved by making the gaps thicker, darker and continuous.

One caution: When drawing these dashes and dots, it's easy to draw too much.

While drawing, stop after every few seconds. Ask yourself whether the wooden effect is

clearly achieved. If yes, stop right there. Avoid the temptation to draw some more.

Remember, less is more!

If you need to draw the wood from close quarters, you will need to add some more details to the texture.

See an example of wood texture in detail below. The texture is divided into the 'waves' using dashes and dots, and the 'eyes of the wood'.

You may add some random marks to indicate scratches and cracks to lend more character to the wood.

Brick Walls

You will need to draw brick walls while illustrating almost any building.

But this doesn't have to be too daunting.

While illustrating a brick wall, note the following characteristics:
a) Bricks are of various sizes.
b) No two bricks placed one above the other are of the same size, and their vertical edges almost never align.
c) Always leave a gap between the adjoining bricks to accommodate the mortar.

The brick wall that I am going to draw here is somewhat rough.

If you look at a modern building, the bricks will be in much better order. But the above principles will still apply.

While adding texture to the brick wall, we need to keep in mind that we need to differentiate between the brick and the mortar. If we use the same texturing technique for both, they both will look the same. We also need to use different shades for both.

Let's apply the shade to the bricks first. I have used various techniques like applying cracks and small indentations over the bricks.

Then we will apply textures to the mortar. A combination of stippling and random strokes is a preferred technique for me here, but you may use either of these.

Stone Walls

A stone wall can be one of the following types (but not limited to those types). I have shown three different types of stone walls below.

These types of walls can be found in the old countryside. The stones are stacked one atop another in no specific pattern. They are bound by dirt.

We start by using a random pattern as shown below.

Points to note:
a) The stones are of random shapes. But every stone is leaning against the other stones around it.

b) A part of each stone will touch other stones around it. But keep some gaps between the stones as well. This gap will contain the dirt holding the stones together.

The principle for differentiating between the stones and the mortar is the same as that for the brick wall. Use lighter values on the stones and darker values on the mortar, or the other way round.

For darker values, I have used a combination of random and stippling strokes. For lighter values, I have used hatching, though stippling can also be used to great effect.

The second type of stone walls we will study are made of flat stones laid over one other with a very small amount of any 'glue' like dirt or cement.

Let's start with illustrating the wall like this. Most of the stones are flat and fit snugly against the others around them. There are also some bigger stones in-between.

Note that the gaps between these stones are filled with very dark values. The stones themselves are textured with horizontal and diagonal pen strokes using a thin-tipped pen.

The third type of stone wall we will see is the one typically seen in fort walls, or the walls of historic monuments seen all over the world.

In this kind of wall, the corner pieces (the left-most stones in the picture above) are somewhat straight and have a defined shape at the outermost edge.

The stones within the wall are of random shapes and there's a gap between every stone and its adjoining stone. This gap will be filled with the mortar.

You can see in the finished picture below that I have used stippling for both the stones and the mortar here.

I could afford to do it here because the shapes of the stones were clearly defined. The stones are sparsely shaded, while the mortar is shaded in a dense manner.

Glass

Illustrating glass is a different challenge. Glass is transparent and reflective at the same time. So, it creates some interesting visual illusions.

As an artist, we have many possibilities and options to draw glass. But I will show you one quick method which I often employ for illustrating glass.

This method is quick and effective for creating the feel of the glass. We will use this method in various demonstrations in this book.

Here, I have shown a window with glass panes and a wooden frame. The place where the glass panes are supposed to be is currently empty. We will draw the glass step by step to get an idea of how to tackle the reflection + transparency challenge.

First, we will draw some diagonal lines as follows.

The general rule of thumb for illustrating these lines are:
a) All the diagonal lines in all the groups must be parallel to each other.
b) In a group, no two lines should be of the same length.
c) Each group of lines should have two, three, or four lines.

Are these rules set in stone? Absolutely not. I am only giving you some guidelines based on the technique I use. You are free to use your own intuition and judgment, and experiment as you wish. Diagonal lines are used to indicate reflections.

If the glass windows occupy a very small part of your illustration, you may want to stop at this stage. It's enough to just indicate a presence of glass on the windows, since it will be surrounded by many other textures like bricks, stones, wood, etc. However, if glass panes of a window are the main subject of your illustration, like the window here, then you will want to go to the step below.

First, determine the objects which are partially visible through the window, or reflected on the window. Draw their rough outlines using a light pencil. In this illustration, these objects are the curtain on the left-hand side and the door inside the room.

Next, shade these objects lightly as shown here using hatching strokes.

You may vary the darkness (value) of each object depending on its distance from the window. The objects near the window will be brighter, and vice versa.

But remember a very important point.

While shading the objects inside the house, leave out the area between the parallel diagonal strokes blank. The shading should be strictly outside this area. This will simultaneously create an effect of a reflective as well as a transparent surface.

The Omnibus of Pen Sketching

Human Figures (In Landscape Illustrations)

Most of the artists I know are daunted by the mere mention of the human figure. Most of the landscape illustrations we see are devoid of any people, and it's no accident!

Human figure illustration is understandably a very challenging subject.

And thankfully, we are not going into the actual illustration of the human figure here.

What we are going to learn is to draw the human figures within our landscape illustrations.

What's the difference? You may ask.

Human figures within the landscape illustrations are somewhat figurative (as in a figurative head of state). They are not meant to mimic the actual humans, but to convey a sense of human presence.

But why do we do this?

Including some human figures in the landscape provides a sense of scale as well as realism to the picture.

In Part 4, we will include human figures in one of our illustrations.

Let's see how we include human figures in the landscapes.

The human figure we draw for the landscapes is termed as a 'perfume bottle figure'. The picture below shows the steps of how the figure should be drawn.

Simple enough?

Now we can use the same principle and just change a few things to manipulate this figure to do anything we want it to do.

Now don't let your imagination run wild! We are talking about landscapes only!

Below, I have given a few examples of what we can do with the human figure. Do you think you can manage to draw something like this? Easy-peasy?

I thought so!

Perspective

The following tips are in no way a comprehensive perspective study. These quick hacks are meant to help you through some of the exercises later in this book.

For the detailed study of perspective, I have written another book, very imaginatively titled 'Composition and Perspective'. You can find it here:

https://HuesAndTones.net/books/cp/

You can also subscribe to my video training on Composition and Perspective here:

https://HuesAndTones.net/ArtTrng/Composition and Perspective.html

I have uploaded many perspective demonstrations to YouTube, which you can watch on my YouTube channel:

https://youtube.com/c/huesandtones/

One-Point Perspective:

When you look at an object from the front, it appears in one-point perspective.

The perspective lines for a one-point perspective are drawn like this. The point where all the perspective lines converge is called the Vanishing Point.

Notice that all the horizontal lines of the doors, windows, and roofs align with the perspective lines. The vertical lines remain perpendicular to the horizon.

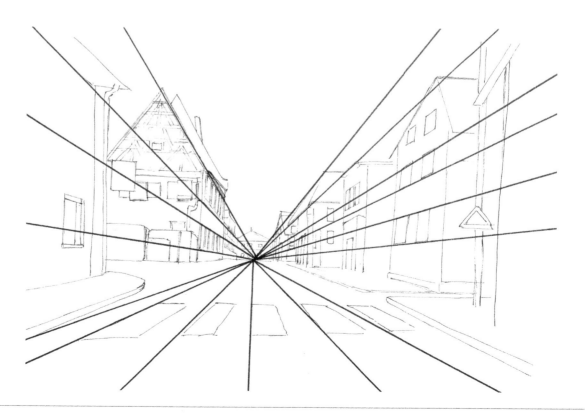

The Omnibus of Pen Sketching

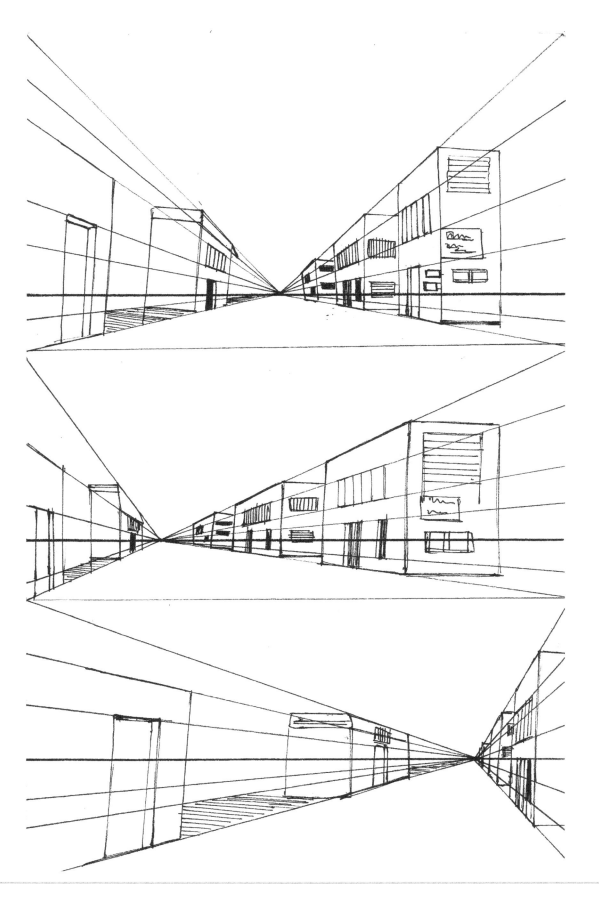

Two-Point Perspective:

We will use the two-point perspective concepts in some of the upcoming exercises.

When we can see two surfaces of an object at the same time, we are watching that object in two-point perspective.

We draw two sets of perspective lines for two-point perspective illustration, considering two vanishing points, one on each side of the object.

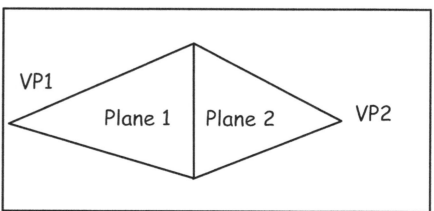

The Omnibus of Pen Sketching

The perspective lines look like this:

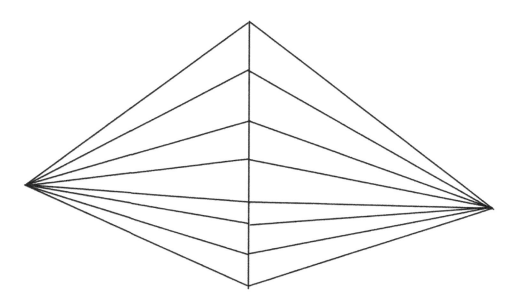

And the object itself will align with the perspective lines like this:

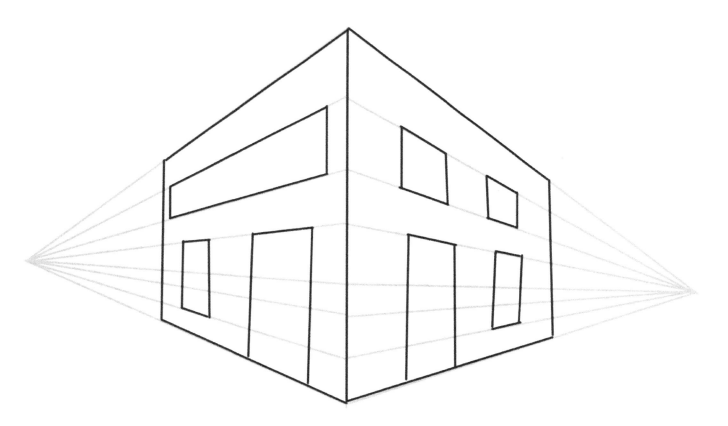

Let's start with a few simple exercises using pens. I assume you have a few technical pens handy for these exercises.

If not, use a ballpoint pen or a gel pen of any color. However, they will not allow fine control over the tip size like the technical pens.

Let's jump in…

PART 2:

SIMPLE

EXERCISES

The various exercises in the 'Simple' part will take you through illustrating some objects like a football, an ice cream cone, a candle, etc. And not only will we draw the object, but we will do some shading as well. Because ultimately, we want to be able to use this knowledge to draw the world around us. Ready?

A Football

Let's draw a football. We have already practiced contour shading techniques in 'Get-Set-Sketch'. Now it's time to put this technique to the test!

Start with a simple circle. Use a rounder tool or the lid of a jar, or any creative tool you can think of to draw this circle.

Just make sure you draw this circle very lightly using a pencil. The circle is shown with a darker outline here than it should be, only for your understanding.

Draw dots as shown below to mark the points where the black panels on the ball will meet. Use very light marks. The dots shown here are intentionally drawn dark for your easy understanding only.

Start connecting the dots as shown. Note that the lines connecting these dots are not straight but run along the contour of the spherical shape of the ball.

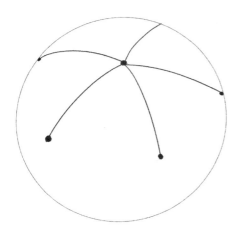

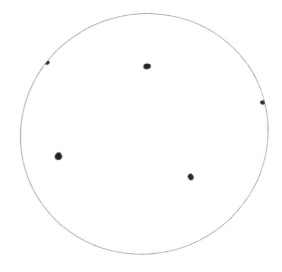

Complete drawing the lines as shown below.

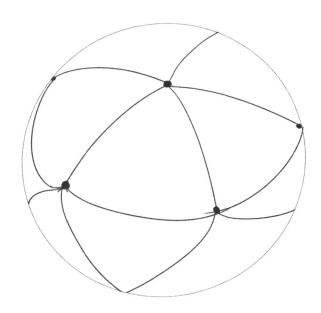

Now we will draw the first panel over the football. It's a matter of simply joining the lines as shown.

The lines of the pentagon should be drawn slightly curved.

Remember, these lines are present over a curved surface, and they will bend in tandem with the surface.

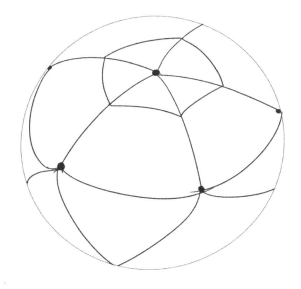

Completely cover the pentagon with black color. You may use a brush pen to lend a solid black color as shown here, or you may use dense cross-hatching to achieve the same effect.

If you choose to use cross-hatching, make sure that every horizontal/vertical/diagonal stroke is along the contour of the sphere, not straight.

Draw the rest of the panels as shown below. Observe that some of the panels are only partially visible to us from this perspective.

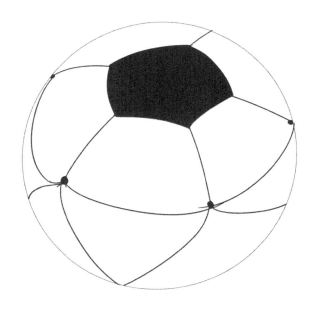

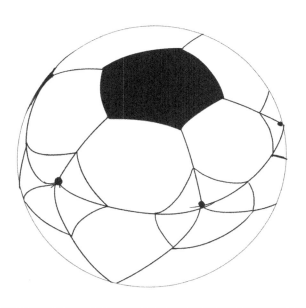

Fill all the panels with solid black color as shown. If you use cross-hatching to darken these areas, remember the instructions given a couple of steps ago.

While shading with cross-hatching, follow the contour of the sphere over which the panels are residing.

Now add some contour shading using a technical pen to the white parts of the football as shown.

Add some contour shading using a white ballpoint pen over the black parts to indicate a slight shine on the surface.

The Omnibus of Pen Sketching

An Ice Cream Cone

Let's draw this delicious looking ice cream cone using pens. The picture on the left-hand side shows the rough shape of the ice cream dollop and the areas of the light and shadow.

The picture on the right-hand side is the one we are aiming for. However, since the shape of the ice cream dollop is quite unpredictable, you have a lot of leeway while drawing it. Just make sure it's somewhat round shaped at the top.

Start with a simple cone shape like this (left). I have drawn this shape with dark lines only for your easy reference. But you must draw it very lightly using an HB pencil.

Drawing lightly at this stage will help us correct any mistakes we may make.

Draw an oval like this (right) over the cone. The horizontal line at the top of the cone should form the diameter of this oval.

Draw an ice cream dollop like this. You may take as much liberty as you want while drawing this shape. If it shows even a little resemblance to a round shape at the top, you are all set!

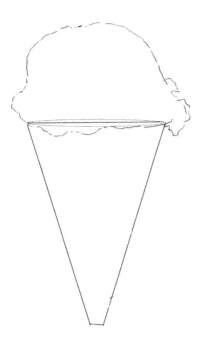

Draw the intersecting horizontal lines like these. Again, these lines must run along with the round contour shape of the cone.

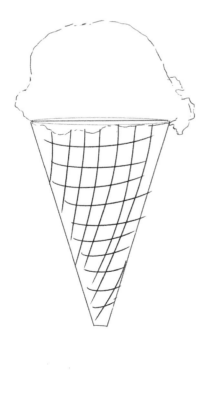

Draw lines over the cone-like those shown on the right. Again, you do not have to be very accurate here, as these lines will vary as per the type of the cone.

Just make sure that the lines follow the round contour shape of the cone. Do not draw them as straight lines, else the cone will look flat.

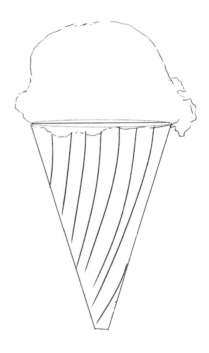

Add the outline for the shadow and light area as shown below. Use a light pencil for drawing this outline. The words shown over the cone are for your reference only!

The Omnibus of Pen Sketching

Add details to the cone. Here, I have used hatching to indicate shadows over the cone. The boundaries of the shadow were already marked as shown on the previous page.

For the dollop of ice cream, I have used mostly stippling. One good thing about the dollop is that you may choose to do as much or as little detailing on it as you wish.

I have chosen to use stippling for shading over most of the dollop. You are free to use a shading method and level of detail of your choice.

A Plain Candle and a Half-Melted Candle

We will learn to draw a simple cylinder-shaped candle as shown on the right-hand side first.

We will generously use cross-hatching and contour shading for illustrating this candle.

Then we will learn to draw a partially melted candle shown on the left-hand side. This will

be especially fun to draw. We will learn to draw abstract shapes like the melted parts of the candle, as well as learn to create some wonderful shading effects using minimal contour strokes.

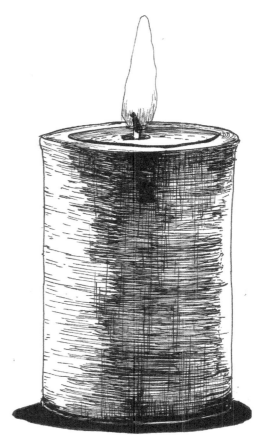

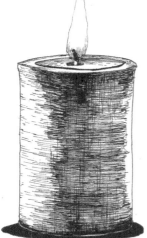

Let's draw this candle first.

Let's begin by drawing a simple flask-like shape like this. Note that the bottom of this flask is a semi-circle. Make sure not to draw it as a straight line.

The Omnibus of Pen Sketching

Draw the top part of the cylinder as shown below. Keep a small gap between the far end of the oval. We will use this gap to draw the wick and the flame.

Remember that in a pen illustration, it's difficult if not impossible to draw over the parts already drawn. So, it's prudent to plan the overlapping elements as much as we can and leave empty spaces accordingly.

Draw another oval within the first oval like this. This inner oval should roughly follow the contours of the outer oval. But one does not necessarily need to be very accurate here (I'm not!).

Draw another small circle at the center of the inner circle and draw the wick through it as follows (first picture). Since this is a burning candle, the wick will be partially blackened at the top.

Draw the flame (middle picture). For a better visual composition, I have shown the direction of the flame slightly at an angle to the wick. This is not a necessity. You may take as much

liberty as you want while drawing the shape and the angle of the flame.

I have also drawn a few contour lines below the inner edge of the circle to thicken that area.

Now start drawing the contour lines as shown below (last picture).

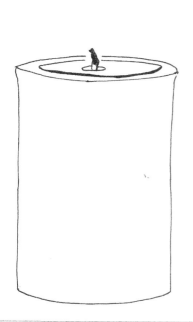

Here (first picture), I have marked some area on the right-hand side using small contour strokes. I will use this area to depict some highlight by avoiding shading it.

Avoiding the area marked for highlight, draw contour strokes as shown below (middle picture). Notice that I have kept a large area on the left-hand side untouched as well. The goal is to depict the darkest shadows in the middle part, and highlights on the left- and right-hand sides.

Thicken the shading in the middle part, while continuing the shading over the blank area on the left-hand side (last picture).

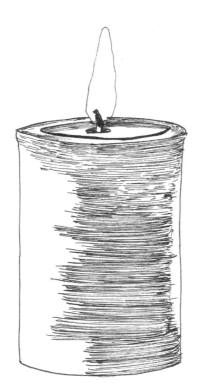

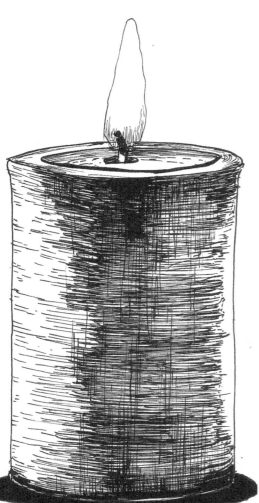

Draw some vertical cross-hatching lines as shown below. These lines should be drawn straight, contrary to the horizontal contour lines.

Draw a thick shadow below the candle to 'ground' it. This shadow will provide a visual clue to the viewer that the candle is resting on the ground. Else the viewer is likely to think that it's floating (or worse, the viewer will be clueless about the whereabouts of the candle).

Now let's draw this candle with melted wax.

Start with a rough outline of the candle as shown below. The original cylindrical shape of the candle is surrounded by the shape of the melted wax.

You may google for some pictures of a candle with melted wax or use a real candle as a model. The shape of the melted parts is completely random, and you don't need to worry about accuracy.

You may download and use the below rough sketch from this web page:

https://HuesAndTones.net/slabreferences/

Mark the darkest areas (First picture). Note that the downward facing parts of the wax lumps are dark as they are facing away from the flame. You may darken some of the areas over the melted wax as shown.

First shade the cylindrical part of the candle using straight hatching strokes (middle picture). These strokes should be denser just below the flame, where the least amount of candlelight will reach.

Use contour strokes to shade the lumps of the melted wax at the back of the candle (last picture). Keep the lumps of wax at the foreground untouched at this stage.

For the lumps of wax at the foreground, use contour strokes very sparingly. This area will receive direct light from the flame above. So, it should be shaded less, just to indicate that there's a surface there.

I decided to add some jazz to the illustration by darkening the background. I did this using a brush pen, as I needed a uniform black color. This step is optional.

A Piece of Fruit

Let's start with an illustration of an apple. We will use different shading techniques to lend texture and shadows to the apple.

You may download and use the rough sketch from this web page:

https://HuesAndTones.net/slabreferences/

Focus only on getting the rough shape to be apple-like. There's no need to fret over accuracy. It's a piece of fruit. It's not supposed to be perfectly shaped like an artificial object.

It will be a very simple illustration of an apple with a little stem. The image below shows the rough outline of the picture. Draw such an outline using a pencil first.

Note: The outline shown below is drawn in a dark value only to give you a clear idea about the shape to draw. When drawing using a pencil, keep the strokes very light, because we will erase them later after the pen work is done.

Draw the darkest areas of the picture, i.e. the shadow immediately below the apple, and a part of the stem. I have used a brush pen for this shading. You may use a brush pen/a fat-tipped technical pen for the same effect.

Lend some texture to the stem using contour strokes.

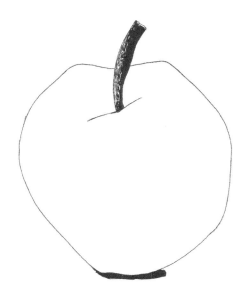

Start defining the shape of the apple using contour strokes.

Continue defining the shape of the apple. Notice that I have placed these strokes in a scattered manner. This serves two purposes.

a) It makes sure the picture does not look too cluttered.

b) Before going into any intricate detailing, we need to define the broad shape first. Keeping the contour strokes scattered makes sure we do not get lost in detail and lose sight of the overall shape.

Also, notice the dark shadow of the stem over the surface of the apple.

Once the broad shape is in place, start increasing the density of contour strokes on the left-hand side of the apple, where the shadows are supposed to be.

We are assuming that the light is falling on the apple from the above and slightly left-hand side. So, the lower part of the apple will face away from the light and will be in shadow. Extend the shadow in this part.

You may see one white space in the lower part of the apple on the left-hand side. It's there for a purpose.

The light falling on the surface on which the apple is resting will get reflected from the lower side of the apple. This will cause this area to look somewhat bright, even though it's in shadow.

The Omnibus of Pen Sketching

Extend the dark shadow below the apple with hatching strokes. Remember the 'Shadows' part from Part 1 of this book? As the shadow goes away from the object, it gets lighter.

From this point, it's up to you how much you want to work on this picture to call it 'finished'. My suggestion would be to leave it here and start with the next exercise.

As we do more exercises, we will keep refining our shading techniques and will draw much more detailed and 'finished' looking illustrations.

A Bottle of Mineral Water

Let's draw a bottle of mineral water. This is a very common (and mundane) subject, I admit.

But as an illustrator, one of our privileges is to find beauty in the most mundane subjects and still make our illustrations pretty!

You may download and use the below rough sketch from this web page:

https://HuesAndTones.net/slabreferences/

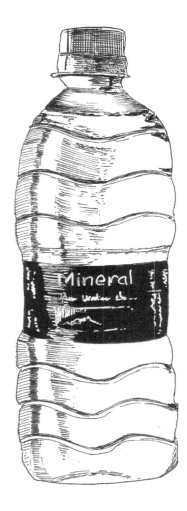

Let's start with an outline of the bottle. It does not have to be exactly symmetrical. We want a hand-drawn look to our illustration, which is key to the beauty of the illustration.

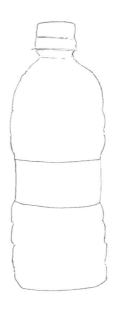

Draw the pattern over the bottle lid using parallel straight lines. Shade the lower part of the lid using stippling.

Draw the upper water level. This should be drawn along the contour of the neck of the bottle.

Completely darken the label over the bottle. We will later use a white ballpoint pen to draw over it.

Draw the segment lines as follows. You may want to draw these lines broken for now. They will be emphasized later.

Shade the part of the bottle above the water level with contour strokes as shown below.

Mark the outlines for shading and highlights along the length of the bottle as shown below. Keep these outlines extremely light and dotted. We don't want these lines showing in the final illustration.

Use contour strokes to shade the area outlined on the left-hand side. Then use slightly denser contour strokes to shade the narrow adjacent area outlined.

Add some thickness to the segment lines from above.

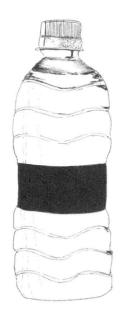

Draw the contour strokes in the middle area as shown. We have kept one band completely white on the left-hand side to indicate a highlight.

Shade the lid of the bottle using cross-hatching contour strokes. Add any finishing touches you find necessary.

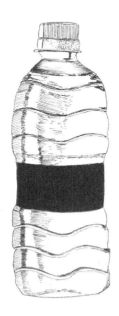

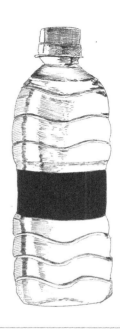

Add some random text and design over the label part of the bottle using a white ballpoint pen.

Continue the highlight from the rest of the bottle onto the label using contour strokes using the white pen.

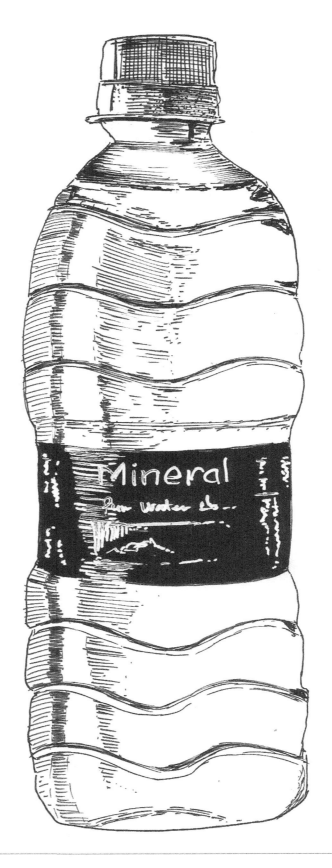

The Omnibus of Pen Sketching

A Leaf

While drawing natural objects like leaves and trees, one has plenty of leeway. You can be as loose and expressive as you want.

You may download and use the below rough sketch from this web page:

https://HuesAndTones.net/slabreferences/

We will start by marking the spine of the leaf as below. At this stage, use a light pencil stroke only.

Draw the outline as follows. Use a pencil to do this initially. We want to draw both halves approximately the same size. After you are satisfied that the shape is okay, trace it with a pen. Now you may put aside the pencil and start drawing with a pen.

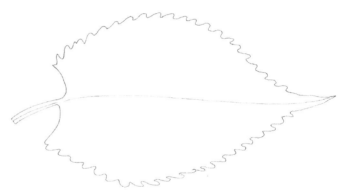

Mark some veins in the leaf as follows. Observe that the adjoining veins do not touch each other over the central spine. They begin a little farther from each other along the spine.

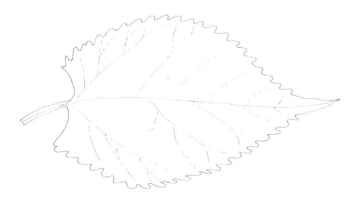

Let's give some volume to these primary veins. Draw one side of each vein thicker than the other side. This will create an illusion of depth.

Complete drawing the primary veins. You may draw as many or as few veins as you want. Just make sure you don't draw too many, else shading will be a nightmare for you!

Start shading the parts between the primary veins as shown here, using the hatching strokes. I have used a thin-tipped pen for these strokes.

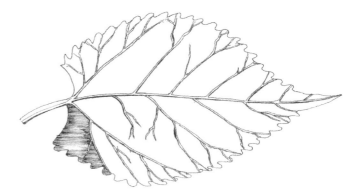

To further darken the area, I have cross hatched this part. We are going to assume that the light is falling on the upper part of the leaf, throwing darker shadows over the bottom part.

Complete the cross-hatching over the entire lower part of the leaf. The shade must be darker near the central vein. Try not to draw over the crisscrossing veins (I know, it's nearly impossible. But don't worry too much about it. We will cover up the mistakes later).

Start shading the upper half of the leaf, with the darkest areas near the central vein.

Complete the cross-hatching of the upper part, like the lower part.

Draw the network of thinner veins using a white ball-point pen. Use the white pen to tidy up the veins drawn earlier.

PART 3: MEDIUM COMPLEXITY EXERCISES

The various exercises in the 'Medium Complexity' part will take you through illustrating some objects and scenes like a staircase, a shopfront, a truck, etc. These objects are made of multiple components, but they are not too complex to draw. Hence, they are classified as 'Medium Complexity'. Ready?

An Old Wooden Door

Old wooden doors like the one shown here are not simply inanimate objects, but they are stories of a bygone era.

Let's use this reference photograph below to draw the wooden door. Such doors have a wealth of textures, making them ideal subjects for pen illustration.

You may download and use the reference photograph and the rough sketch on the next page from this web page:

https://HuesAndTones.net/slabreferences/

While illustrating any real-life object, we need to define its boundaries and relative sizes of the various components within the object.

In this example, if we consider the width of the door as X, the height of the door is approximately 2.5X. This is an approximate size only, calculated visually.

Also, note that the edges of the door are converging as they go away from us. We see this skewed perspective because we are looking at the door slightly from one side, not exactly from the front.

We will first draw a light outline of the door using a pencil, followed by a pen outline using a thin-tipped pen. I prefer to use 0.01 tip size Pigma Micron pen for this purpose.

You may notice that in this picture, some lines are crooked. This is perfectly okay. This is an old door and its weathered wood is supposed to be a little crooked.

In fact, if the lines look too perfect, the illustration will look artificial. That's why I always advocate drawing without using a ruler.

Let's start with marking the darkest areas of the illustration as shown in the pictures below. For this purpose, I use fat-tipped pens such as 0.05 or 0.08 and brush tip pens.

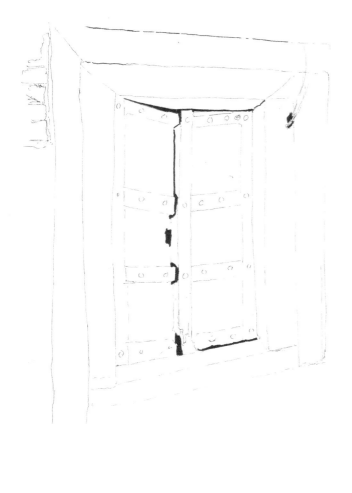

Now let's focus on those areas which are slightly less dark than those we already covered. The inner edges of these doors should be shaded such that they are not completely blacked out.

Do this shading for only the edges facing us. This will induce a nice 3D effect on these edges.

Let's mark a few of the areas on the door where we want to add details such as chipped paint and the torn remains of paper stuck over one of the door panels.

You can also see here that I have extended the darkest areas slightly using some pen shading. This gives a more realistic feel to the shading. In real life, you will rarely see a dark area adjoining a bright area. There's almost always a 'transition area' between them with middle tones.

Let's shade the interior of the frame surrounding the door. I have used cross-hatching for the upper edge. This is the area where the least amount of light will reach.

The right-hand side inner edge of the door frame is made slightly less dark using hatching. The outer edge of the door frame and the threshold will receive the maximum light and are kept without shading. The wooden textures are shown prominently.

Start shading the left-hand edge of the door frame. I have used some stippling here to indicate the weathered wood. Also, the front edge of the threshold is shaded to differentiate it from the upper edge.

Start shading the door panels. We had already marked the areas to shade. We can now simply fill in the shade in those areas. However, be careful not to get carried away and do too much shading. Remember… less is more! Some meager stippling patches will do to indicate a solid surface.

I have used the hatching strokes for the patch of color outside the door frame. If you intend to color this illustration, there's no need to do this.

In fact, this is simply a choice of mine to do this. This is not a rule. You will make many such choices when doing a pen illustration, and almost every one of them will be a correct one if you run with your intuition.

Now it's time to add some finishing touches. You can add any shading you deem necessary. Here, I decided to add some lines diverging from the door outwards to indicate the ground. Drawing the ground provides a context for the door.

shirish

Some Rustic Stairs

Let's use this reference photograph below to draw these rustic stairs. I captured this photograph in the Indian city of Jaipur in Rajasthan state.

Rajasthan is famous for its vast desert landscapes and rustic houses. These brick walls and wooden doors provide excellent opportunities for creating some wonderful textures.

You may download and use the reference photograph and the rough sketch from this web page:

https://HuesAndTones.net/slabreferences/

Let's start with an initial outline as per the reference illustration below. You should draw this very lightly over the paper using an HB pencil.

The diagram below shows the approximate proportions. Getting the proportions right at the beginning itself is important. Once we start with linework, it's easy to get lost in detail and lose a sense of proportion.

Note that the proportions shown here are determined by visually scanning the source photograph, not by using the exact measurements.

Since we are looking at these stairs from an angle, the edges of the stairs will appear to be converging away from us. To make sure these lines appear visually correct, we will draw some perspective lines.

This is a two-point perspective scene since two surfaces of the stairs are visible to us. Please refer to the Two-Point Perspective chapter in Part 1 of this book for details.

But your next question will be… How do I draw

these perspective lines then? I will answer that right away.

Take a printout or a digital copy of the original photograph. Start drawing lines aligning with the top of the stairs, doorframe, etc. These lines will start converging towards the left-hand side. They will converge into a vanishing point.

The vanishing point may be well outside the paper (or screen, if you use a digital copy) on the left-hand side. Don't worry about finding it. We just need to make sure our illustration is in line.

You don't have to be perfect either while drawing these lines. These are only guidelines and should be drawn very lightly. They will be erased later.

Below is the initial illustration drawn using pencils and then traced over with 0.01 tip size Pigma Micron pen. Some lines are deliberately drawn broken. It's better to draw fewer details at this stage to avoid mistakes.

I always start marking the darkest areas first. Of course, this is the way I do things, and it's not the only way or the best way of drawing. You may choose to start with lighter areas first, and you will still be right.

We are aiming for the feel of very bright light over the subject. So, we will keep the contrast high.

Let's focus our attention on the two wooden doors on the right-hand side. Draw some details as shown. The lower edges of the panels of the upper door are made darker. This will induce an effect of depth in the picture.

Now let's draw some brickwork on the wall. Keep it light. I have used a 0.005 tip size pen for these stones. The wall is bathed in blinding sunlight and the textures will appear less prominent. Both the doors are in shadow and their wooden textures will appear very prominent.

Observe that I have used the stippling technique to indicate the rough nature of the wall behind that standing wooden pole. If I had not used some stippling (or any other means of indicating a surface), the wall would appear a blank space.

Let's add some contour hatching strokes to the wall above the upper side door (the image below).

Our aim is to show a deep contrast between the shadowed area on the right-hand side and the brightly lit area on the left-hand side. So, we will draw these contour strokes dense, creating a deep shadow.

Continue shading the wall and the stairs as shown here. Mark the outlines of shadows with pencil first, so that the shadows can be restricted to the edges we have already decided.

I finished the illustration by adding some texture to the wall on the right-hand side (above the lower door) and completing the shading. You are free to add any finishing touches you deem necessary. Use your intuition here.

A Small Boat

While on a vacation in Goa, India, I spotted this small boat from a bridge. The rustic nature of the boat, along with the calm water around it, was enticing. Let's learn how to draw this boat illustration.

We will use this reference photograph to draw this boat.

You may download and use the reference photograph and the rough sketch from this web page:

https://HuesAndTones.net/slabreferences/

Draw a rough outline as shown below using light pencil strokes. The aim is only to block the broad shapes, not add any details.

Now take the pen (I used a brush pen for this) and draw the foreground foliage on the left-hand side as a silhouette. This creates an excellent framing for the boat illustration.

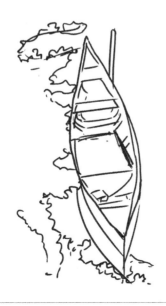

The Omnibus of Pen Sketching

Draw the initial boat outline as shown below (first picture).

Complete the boat outline (middle picture). The broken lines drawn below the bow of the boat mark the area for drawing the reflection of the boat.

Mark the darkest areas within the boat illustration. I prefer to use a brush pen to mark the darkest areas. You may use a brush pen/a fat-tipped technical pen for achieving the same effect.

Shade the interior of the boat using contour strokes. Draw wood texture. The boundaries of these shadows were marked beforehand using light pencil lines so that the shading is precise.

We need to darken the internal part of the boat so that it transitions well from the darkest parts to the lightest parts. We use cross-hatching strokes for the shadows adjacent to the darkest parts.

Now shade the external part of the hull. Shade the reflections using hatching.

Now it's time to add some finishing touches. Draw the ripples in the water. The ripples should be drawn sparingly since this is very calm water. I have used both black technical pens and a white ballpoint pen to add the finishing touches.

A Banyan Tree Trunk

Banyan trees are my favorite subjects to draw due to their complex root system and the abundance of textures they offer.

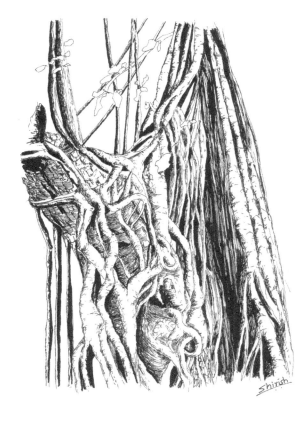

We will use the below reference photograph to draw this illustration.

You may download and use the reference photograph and the rough sketch from this web page:

https://HuesAndTones.net/slabreferences/

Let's start with a rough outline of the banyan tree. You don't need to be too accurate while doing this. As long as you manage to get the overall shape correct, it's okay. We will draw this outline lightly using a pencil, and then trace over it with a thin-tipped technical pen when we are satisfied with the overall structure.

As always, start with shading the darkest areas first. Normally, the areas facing downward are the darkest. We are assuming that the light is falling diagonally from the right-hand side onto the tree, so most of the shadows will be on the left-hand side and downward.

Start adding texture to the big stem on the left-hand side. You may use contour shading or the method I have used here to draw the texture.

Shade the stem on the left-hand side using contour strokes. Beware that there's a huge risk of visual clutter in this illustration. We want the viewer to clearly identify various areas in the picture. We will do this using different values for different parts of the illustration.

Because of shading the main branch, see how the overlapping roots are now clearly visible over the stem.

Add texture to the branches on the left-hand side. Since the light will fall on these branches diagonally from the right-hand side, the values grow progressively darker towards the left-hand side.

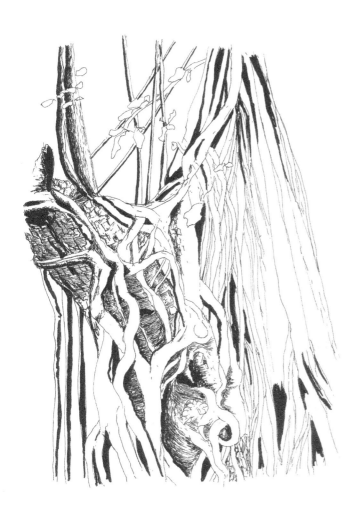

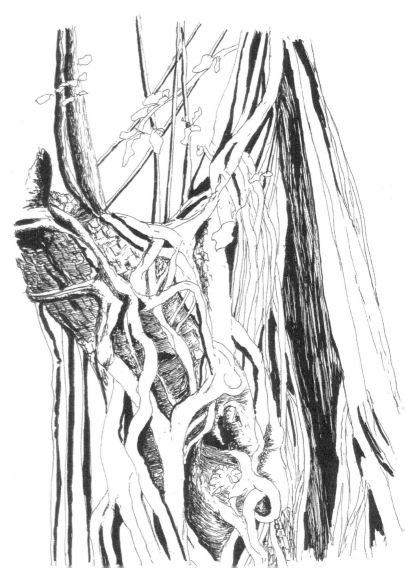

Now we will focus on the bunch of roots receding in the small cove on the right-hand side. The goal is to make this bunch dark, but still visible enough. For this, we will use dense contour strokes. The dark shade will create an illusion that the bunch of roots is receding.

Start adding texture to the overlapping roots over the main stem. Use contour strokes. But do not make them too dense. Direct light will fall on these roots, and texture will be visible only for the sides which are turning away from the light (on the left-hand side).

Keep adding a light texture to the roots on the left-hand side.

Add texture to the rest of the branches, keeping the same principle above in mind… Light texture to the areas facing away from the light, no texture to the areas directly exposed to the light.

Add any finishing touches you may want to add.

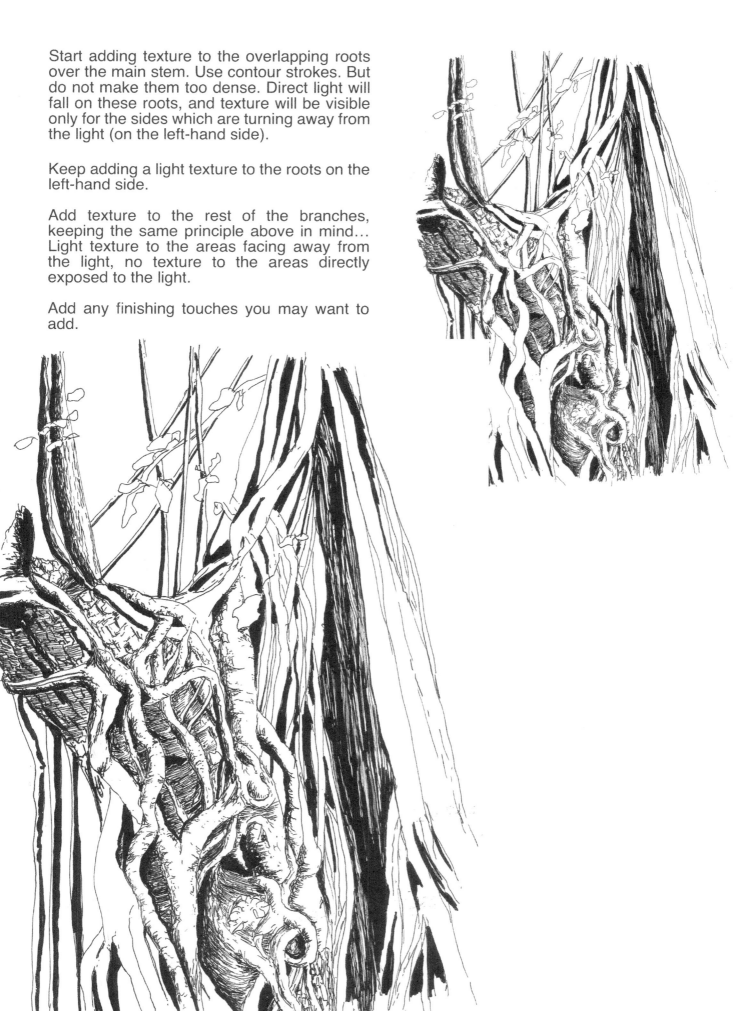

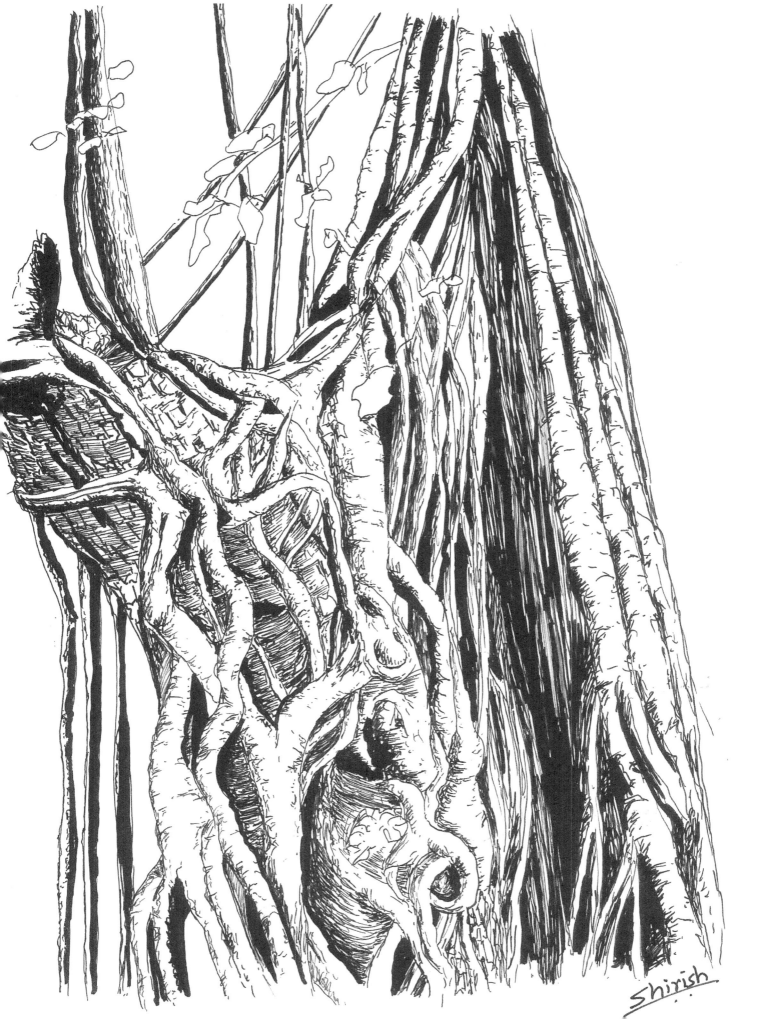

A Shrine

While visiting a local temple, I came upon this rustic shrine. The simple, yet elegant shape and the weathered look of the shrine instantly qualified it as a perfect subject for a pen illustration!

Let's draw this shrine step-by-step.

You may download and use the reference photograph and the rough sketch from this web page:

https://HuesAndTones.net/slabreferences/

As usual, start with a rough outline of the shrine using a light pencil stroke. Once you are satisfied with the pencil work, proceed with tracing over the pencil lines with a thin-tipped technical pen.

Mark the darkest areas. I have used a brush pen for this. You may use a brush pen/a fat-tipped technical pen for this purpose.

Draw the basil plant above the shrine. Basil plant is a natural air purifier and can be seen at the entrance of many temples.

Use random strokes to draw the basil plant leaves. No need to add too many details.

Draw the dark shadowed area within the inner part of the shrine. Use hatching or cross-hatching stokes. The goal is to show this area as very dark, but without eliminating all the details completely as we did for the darkest areas.

Now let's shade the remaining area within the shrine such that it's somewhat less dark than the area marked before and will show the stone texture.

The inside of the shrine is made of the irregular, yet smooth stone surface. The smoothness of the surface is partly due to the elements, and partly due to the oil and milk poured over the stone idol as an offering. We will use stippling to texture this surface.

Draw shadowed areas at the base of the shrine using stippling (for stone surface) and hatching (for shading).

I have used broken pen strokes as shown here to indicate the weathered surfaces of the upper part of the shrine. You may do all kinds of experiments here for texturing. Just make sure you keep enough white spaces. It's very easy to get carried away and fill up the entire area, which will make it look ugly, rather than elegant.

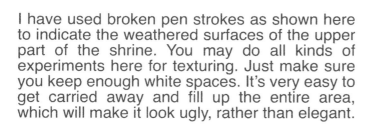

The Omnibus of Pen Sketching

Start stippling the left and right-hand sides of the shrine. Since we have used a lot of stippling over the other areas, we will keep our stippling in this area minimal.

This minimal stippling will create a sense of a surface on these sides while creating an illusion that this area is getting more incident light than the dark areas marked earlier.

Shade the stone flower and the plant pot above the shrine. Use shading sparingly, and keep some white spaces as shown. I have shown some cracks emerging at the top of the plant pot, giving it a weathered look.

Lightly shade the stone idols within the shrine. Add any finishing touches you may feel you should add.

A Shopfront

I did this illustration of a beautiful shopfront in Mount Airy, NC, USA using a reference photograph shared with me by a FB friend, Emi.

Let's draw this shopfront.

You may download and use the reference photograph and the rough sketch from this web page:
https://HuesAndTones.net/slabreferences/

Before beginning to draw the shopfront, we need to find out the relative proportions of the various objects within the picture. We can visually divide the shopfront into three sections.
• The upper section consisting entirely of brickwork.
• The middle section with glass panes.
• The lower section where the shop is located.

For simplifying the illustration, and to keep everything within the page, let's divide the storefront building as shown below. Remember that these are approximate measurements. We are doing an expressive illustration here, not an architectural illustration!

X, Y, and Z represent lengths of the various parts of the shop building.

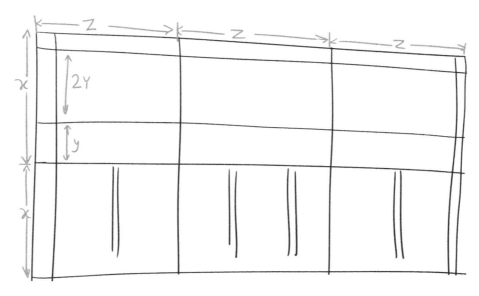

As you can see, the complete building is horizontally divided into two equal parts (represented by X). The lower part contains the door and the glass front, while the upper part contains the windowpanes above and the brick wall part of the front of this building.

The upper X is further divided into the windowpanes (represented by Y) and the brick part (2Y). The brick part is approximately twice as tall as the windowpane part.

Vertically, the building is divided into three

equal parts, each represented by Z.

Once we have established the measurements as above, we can now draw a rough pencil sketch mimicking these measurements. Below, you can see a preliminary sketch with the boundaries marked.

Note that even though this subject is quite heavy on straight lines, I have not used a ruler for drawing them. Let the lines look organic and hand drawn. That is where the true beauty of an illustration lies.

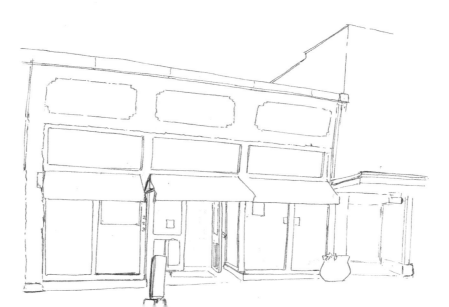

We will start with the canopies. The patterns over the cloth of these canopies lend a certain character to the shopfront. First, draw the patterns on the left and right canopies only.

Observe on the left side canopy how I have marked the left, right and middle stripes first. This makes sure that the stripes that we will draw align properly with the edges.

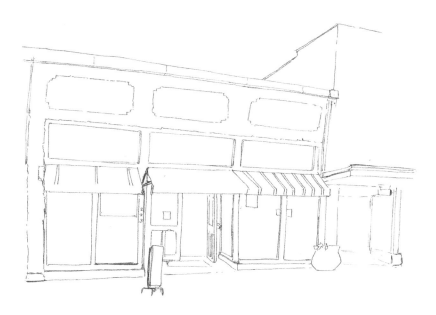

While drawing such patterns, the danger is to get carried away and realize much later that we have missed the symmetry of the pattern.

Like this.

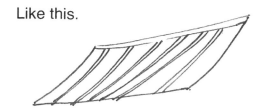

To avoid this, I always draw the lines at various intervals first. Then close these intervals with more lines like this.

Now let's finish illustrating the left/right canopies and the shopfront windows on the left and right. Do not touch the middle canopy as of now. It will soon become clear why.

I have used a brush pen to darken the parts. However, you may use heavy cross-hatching

to achieve the same effect if you like.

Observe the wooden frame of the glass panes on the right-hand side. All the left-hand edges of the wooden frames are thickened. This gives a 3D effect to the wooden frame.

Now we come to the middle canopy. As you can observe in the reference photograph, some strong sunlight is falling directly over the upper part of this canopy.

Since we cannot draw the sunlight with pens, we need to represent this sunlight and the resultant brightness by other means. This can be done by darkening the area around the bright area and using minimum pen strokes in the bright area.

It's now time to draw the glass panes. This is an especially challenging part because the glass is transparent and reflective at the same time. So, we can see some of the stuff within the building through the glass. Simultaneously, some reflections from the street appear on the glass.

We will start with the upper windowpanes. For the stuff visible through the glass, we will use some familiar shapes like the shopping trolleys, but we will break the shapes using some diagonal reflection lines as shown.

We will use some random shapes only to provide a feel of the transparency of the glass panes.

First, draw a very light horizontal line using pencil over the middle canopy, approximately dividing the slanting part into two equal (upper, and lower) halves. We will make the upper part dark and the lower part light. The part of the canopy turning downward is still in the shadow and will have completely dark stripes.

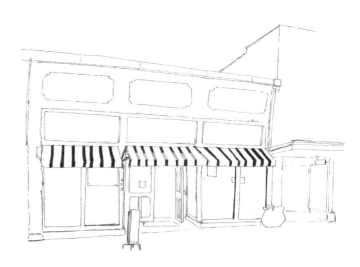

Throughout all this, we must remember a very important point. We must use plenty of white space to indicate the shine of the plate glass.

The Omnibus of Pen Sketching

Now do the same to the glass panes for the shop display windows on the ground floor and the shop door.

The letters 'Sunshine' and the logo over the right-hand side pane are painted over the glass. They will be unaffected by the reflections in the glass.

We are now done with the basic illustration. Now it's time to add some shadows, textures and finishing touches.

The inside of the shop mostly appears dark from our point of view, so we will first add some shadows there.

We will add some wood texture to the door frame, before adding shadows to it.

Then we will add shadows to the sloping part and the forward-facing part of all three canopies. Take care to avoid shading the brightly lit part marked over the middle canopy.

It's now time to draw the brick walls on this building and the surrounding buildings. The goal here is to draw just enough attention to the brick wall without taking the attention away from the shop front. So, we have kept the brick texture to a minimum.

Draw a light shadow on the ground using hatching strokes. This firmly 'grounds' the shop and provides a sense of solidity to the structure.

You may want to mark the boundary for this shadow with a light pencil beforehand.

Use a white ballpoint pen to draw the 'Open' sign at the front of the door.

Feel free to add any finishing touches you want, and we are done!

The Omnibus of Pen Sketching

A Truck

While driving in an isolated stretch of a road in my city, I came across this truck parked on the side of the road. The truck was standing among some overgrown grass and seemed like a neglected piece of machinery.

At first, I thought that it was an abandoned vehicle. But when I drove by the same spot after a couple of days, the truck was gone. Someone had decided to drive it after all!

We will use this reference photograph of the truck to draw the illustration above.

You may download and use the reference photograph and the rough sketch from this web page:

https://HuesAndTones.net/slabreferences/

The shape of the truck creates an excellent contrast against the foliage in the foreground.

But at the same time, all that overlapping makes illustrating this truck especially challenging, doesn't it?

But worry not, we will see how to not just survive but thrive using this overlap.

Shall we begin?

Let's start by understanding how the planes of the truck are juxtaposed against one another. Look at the picture below. The various arrows represent the straightness/curve of the planes of the truck.

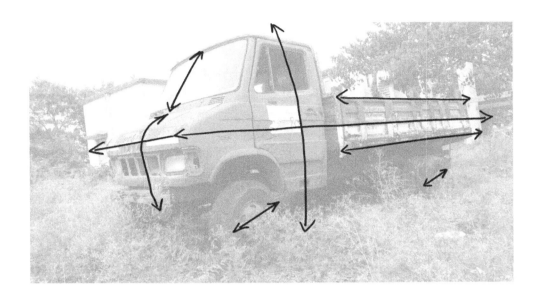

We will draw a rough outline of the truck very lightly using a pencil. The picture below shows the outline for your reference.

This is the first draft of the illustration done on paper using a pen. Note that I have not yet drawn the inner parts of the truck visible through the windshield, and the bottom-most part of the truck.

The bottom part of the truck is partly obscured with grass and weeds. While doing a pen illustration, we must start with the overlapping parts first. So, we will begin with the grass.

Below, I have drawn some grass and weeds at the base of the truck. In addition to providing an environment for the truck to reside, it creates an interesting foreground for the illustration.

If you find this foreground too intimidating, no worries.

You may simply draw a general outline of the foliage and still, it will look good.

Remember, there are no rules in art!

For simplifying drawing the abstract shapes of the foliage, I have zoomed in on the foliage part in these three pictures. You may use these as a reference for illustrating the foliage.

When drawing a pen illustration, I always start from the part which will be dark/less prominent. In the case of this illustration, it's the bed of the truck.

You can see the dark parts marked on the next page.

Focusing initially on the less prominent parts of the illustration helps cover up any mistakes I make at the beginning of the illustration.

And believe me, I make a lot of mistakes!

By the time I come to the prominent subjects within the illustration, my mind and fingers are sufficiently warmed up and nimble. This makes it possible to avoid making too many mistakes later.

Of course, as with all the illustrations in this book and every other book of mine, this statement comes with a disclaimer:

This is my way of illustrating. It does not mean you must do it this way. You are free to do what you find convenient and effective.

Now let's start with the outline of the front cabin of the truck. Note that I have avoided drawing finished outlines for all the parts of the front cabin.

If needed, we can always finish a part using dark lines later. But we cannot erase the dark lines once drawn. So, keep that instinct to cover all surfaces with dark lines in check.

Let's darken the lower part of the truck, which is in shadow. We will completely black out some part and use the shading techniques like hatching and cross-hatching for some parts where grey shades are needed.

The Omnibus of Pen Sketching

Now we will shade the underside of the wooden planks running across the length of the truck bed and add some texture to the wood.

To differentiate the planks from the wood surrounding them, I have used two different texture strokes on these two parts.

While the texture lines on the wooden planks are horizontal, the texture lines on the surrounding wood are vertical to the planks. This helps in visually separating the planks and the surface underneath.

You can see in the picture below how some minimal amount of shading can create an illusion of shape and depth for the main body of the truck. Here, I have used a combination of hatching and stippling to shade various metal parts.

Notice that I have also lightly drawn the various paper pamphlets stuck over the body of the truck. These are drawn such that they follow the contour of the surface on which they are stuck.

In this case, stippling can create the feel of a rough or rusted piece of metal.

Now it's time to draw the most challenging part, the windshield of the truck.

The windshield is reflective as well as transparent, making it especially tricky to draw. Apply too little shading, and it may look empty. Add even a bit more shading than necessary, and it'll look totally transparent.

But fear not! There's a way to shade this glass. You just need to keep in mind a very important point… less is more!

If you need to choose between more shading and less shading, always choose less.

Here, I have used the hatching (along the contours of the windshield) to shade. But observe how I have liberally kept white spaces cutting through the hatching strokes.

This creates an illusion of reflection. The light hatching strokes create the illusion of transparency.

After reaching this point, it's totally up to you which other finishing touches you might want to apply.

There are no rules for this. But there's always a danger of going overboard and spoiling a perfectly neat illustration in our over-enthusiasm.

So, when you get that question in your mind the first time… Should I keep making changes further? just say No very firmly and stop right there.

If it sounds much easier to say than to do it, it is. But still...

Remember, a work of art is never finished, it's abandoned (The artists stops working on it)!

An Abandoned Car

While visiting the famous Baga beach of North Goa, India, I came across this car abandoned along the roadside. It was already getting encroached with weeds.

Such vehicles are ideal for pen drawing due to their varied textures, as well as the interesting juxtaposition of artificial shapes and natural shapes.

We will use this reference photograph to do the illustration shown above.

You may download and use the reference photograph and the rough sketch from this web page:

https://HuesAndTones.net/slabreferences/

The Omnibus of Pen Sketching

Let's start with this rough sketch. The aim of this rough sketch is to get the proportions right and have an approximation of the scope of this illustration.

Use light pencil strokes to draw the rough sketch.

I have shown some perspective lines below to show you how the edges of the car are aligned. We will not go into the details of perspective illustration at this stage. However, these lines will help you to make sure your illustration is aligned properly to the shape of the car.

Please refer to the section 'One-Point Perspective' in Part 1 of this book for how to draw the perspective lines.

Medium Complexity Exercises

We will start the pen illustration by drawing the overlapping foliage. While drawing a pen illustration, it's more convenient to draw the overlapping elements first.

Ignore the liquor bottle and the bamboo from the photograph!

As an illustrator, it's completely in our control what we should include in the illustration and what we should leave out.

I left out the bamboo and the liquor bottle because I did not feel they were necessary for the subject in hand. If you feel they should be included, go ahead and include them. There's no right or wrong way in art.

Draw the windows on the right-hand side and the windshield. Don't try to draw the lines too straight. Remember, this is a derelict car, and the edges of the windows have been terribly affected by the elements.

Draw the steering wheel and the seats. Again, creating a feel of the elements we are illustrating is enough. No need to be very precise.

Draw the front side of the car as shown. You may feel that this is a bit complicated. If so, use the reference image to trace over.

Draw the right-hand side doors and wheels. While drawing the doors, keep a little gap between the front edge of the front door and the car body, since the car body is dented inwards a bit. The car tires are flat, and the wheels touch the ground.

Draw some grass blades and pebbles on the ground where the wheels are touching. This will make the car look properly 'grounded'.

Let's start by marking the darkest areas. Notice that I have not completely covered the car seat with black. Keep some white spaces there to indicate the light falling on those seats.

I have used a brush pen to mark the darkest areas. You may use a brush pen or a fat-tipped pen to achieve the same effect.

Let's lend some texture to the car bumper. This car is rusting, and its paint is chipping off. So, a rough texture will work here.

The contour strokes at the tip of the bonnet area help establish the shape of the bonnet.

Now shade the front side of the car. Add some dark areas below the bumper, so the edges of the car are better defined.

Add some shading to the car seat using contour strokes. See how I have kept the upper edge of the seat unshaded, so it looks like the light is directly falling there.

Add some finishing touches. Add rust texture to the bonnet. You may use hatching strokes as I have shown below or stippling to indicate rust.

Similarly, add some texture to the side doors, and tires.

And we are done!

PART 4: COMPLEX EXERCISES

The various exercises in the 'Complex' part will take you through illustrating some objects and scenes like a church, a complete landscape from a city, a house in the mountains, etc. These scenes are complex to draw. For drawing them, one not only needs to look at the object but also its relationship and proportions with the various surrounding objects. Ready?

An Old Victorian Building

Let's draw this Victorian-era stone building nestled amongst some lush greenery.

We will use this reference photograph to draw this illustration.

You may download and use the reference photograph and the rough sketch from this web page:

https://HuesAndTones.net/slabreferences/

Just like the old door that we saw in one of the previous examples; such old stone buildings offer a wealth of texture. Even though the overlapping foliage would seem like a hindrance to many-an-illustrator out there, it's an excellent opportunity!

How? You may ask.

Let me enlighten you, my dear fellow illustrator.

The basis of a pen illustration (or any illustration, for that matter) is contrast.

The contrast of black lines against the white spaces.

The contrast of vertical lines against horizontal lines.

The contrast of natural shapes against artificial shapes.

In this example, the natural random shapes of the foliage provide an excellent juxtaposition against the artificial shape of the building.

The foliage also creates a 'Frame within the frame' effect, which is a very powerful compositional element. You can learn in-depth about the topic of composition and perspective in my other, very imaginatively named book, 'Composition and Perspective'.

https://HuesAndTones.net/books/cp/

This picture is a two-point perspective scene. You can find more information about two-point perspective in Part 1 of this book under the 'Perspective' section.

Let's get cracking!

The outline on the next page shows the rough measurements of the building. Such guidelines are always helpful when illustrating complex subjects. It helps break down the complex subject into simpler, manageable chunks.

Note that these measurements are approximate, not to the scale. We are going to draw an expressive illustration here, not an architectural illustration.

Copy this rough outline very lightly on paper using an HB pencil. While drawing, keep comparing with the original photograph to make sure you are on track.

Trace over the rough pencil sketch using a thin-tipped Pigma Micron pen. The dotted, broken lines are deliberate. Drawing such lines allows us to cater for any overlapping elements, as well as correct any initial mistakes.

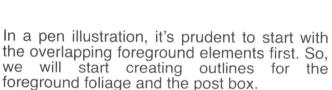

In a pen illustration, it's prudent to start with the overlapping foreground elements first. So, we will start creating outlines for the foreground foliage and the post box.

We are not going to add any details to the foliage. Our focus will entirely be the building, while the foliage will act as a frame for the building illustration.

Let's draw the top arches of this building. These are some of the tougher parts of the illustration due to their unique angles.

Carefully observe the angles of the arches. If you are not sure you can get them right the first time, use the rough sketch provided to trace over.

Add deep shadows to the upper windows and draw outlines for the pillars around the arches.

Draw the stonework over the dome and parapet below the upper windows. Here I have made a small mistake in drawing the left-hand side parapet. The parapet is leaning downward more than it should be. But no worries… we will correct this mistake going forward.

Draw the stonework for the pillars below the top arches. Keep these lines very light and broken. We don't want to add too many details here yet.

Observe that I haven't drawn a single line completely straight. This is a deliberate choice. These pillars are made of stones, and they are quite old. So, these walls and pillars will always form slightly wobbly lines.

Here you can see my first attempt at correcting the perspective of the left-hand side parapet. I have started adding some dark shadows to gloss over the incorrect perspective.

Add some details to the windows and start working on the horizontal stripes straddling the corner of the building. The lower edges of these stripes are made thicker to induce a depth. But do not draw these stripes where the fence is overlapping them as of now.

Work on the fence now. There's no need to add too many details. Some diagonally crisscrossing lines are all that is needed. Observe that I haven't even bothered to draw these lines unbroken.

Since we do not want to draw too much attention to any object other than the building itself, we will keep the details to a minimum everywhere else. Very lightly, complete the remaining horizontal stripes overlapped by the fence using broken lines.

Now it's time to focus on the stonework of the building. The lines of the stones should be parallel to the horizontal stripes straddling the corner.

Just like the stonework for the dome and the arches, keep the detailing to a minimum and use a thin-tipped pen to draw this stonework.

Add some dark shadows to the windows and archway at the ground level.

Observe that the archway on the left-hand side is made completely dark above the fence level. But some random white spaces are left in the area of the archway overlapped by the fence. If this is not done, it would look as if the archway is in front of the fence.

Add some shading to the top dome using contour strokes. The rough stone texture is depicted using stippling for the arches and their pillars. Stippling is used minimally to avoid clutter. Some of the stones over the walls are lightly shaded to add some variation.

Now carefully shade one side of the building using hatching strokes for added contrast. This automatically makes the viewer's eye believe that the left-hand side of the building is in shadow, while the right-hand side is brightly lit. It also adds a nice depth to the picture.

After the illustration was almost complete, I decided to add details to this foreground post box. Use the same lighting angle as the building to the post box, and we are done with this illustration.

You will also notice how the initial perspective mistake is now completely hidden. Would you have noticed it if I had not pointed it out to you? This is the exact point I mentioned in 'The fear of Making Mistakes' section at the beginning of the book.

An Old Telephone

A few weeks ago, I visited a café in a mall near my office. The café was decorated in a retro theme. This ancient model telephone caught my attention.

I quickly clicked a couple of pictures and kept them for referencing later.

We will now use these reference photographs to draw this charming piece of equipment.

You may download and use the reference photograph and the rough sketch from this web page:

https://HuesAndTones.net/slabreferences/

Let's start with this rough sketch. Notice that the phone is drawn slightly tilted as per the original photograph. We will make sure it does not look out of place while drawing the shadows at the end. Till then, please hold your guns!

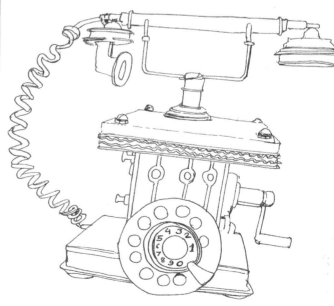

The Omnibus of Pen Sketching

Mark the darkest areas over the instrument. Although most of the surface of this instrument is covered in a matt finish material, it's a little lustrous everywhere. A lustrous surface can be indicated by drawing very dark areas right next to the very bright areas.

Use crisscross lines to draw the fine mesh behind the dial.

Darken the area over the handle of the receiver, leaving one thin strip of white along its length. Pay attention to the upper and lower edges of this strip of white. The edges are made jagged on purpose. This creates a leather-like texture over the handle.

I have used stippling to indicate the rough, matt leather texture over the base of the phone. You may use the method I have used, or you can use the same method we used for the handle of the receiver.

Draw crisscross lines between the jagged lines over the base of the cradle. Make the rest of the area around those jagged lines dark.

I have used the hatching lines over the dial running along its circumference. The idea is to show a matt texture while keeping it different from the other matt textures

I could have used stippling to show a matt finish metal surface. But it would not look different from the other surfaces where we have used stippling to indicate a leather texture.

This is an important lesson: If you used a shading method to apply a texture to one kind of surface, it doesn't mean this method is now set in stone. When choosing a shading method, always consider it in conjunction with the other surfaces within the illustration.

The shading method used for a surface is less

important than the contrast it creates with the other surfaces.

Shade the vertical metal base of the cradle as shown on the right (below left).

Shade the microphone and earpiece (below right). We want to shade them enough to show a matt texture. But at the same time, we want to leave enough white space to show some luster. Add some shadows at the base of the cradle, and add any finishing touches you want, and we are done with the illustration!

The Omnibus of Pen Sketching

A Church

Let's draw this beautiful church building. This illustration is drawn using a reference photograph from Mount Airy, NC, USA, shared with me by a FB friend, Emi.

Let's use this reference photograph to draw the church.

You may download and use the reference photograph and the rough sketch from this web page:

https://HuesAndTones.net/slabreferences/

Let's understand the proportions of this building. The approximate proportions for various parts of the building are shown below.

These are not architectural proportions, but they are measured visually for the purpose of this illustration.

Below is the initial outline sketch of the church. I have used 0.01 tip size Pigma Micron pen to draw this outline.

While drawing this outline, the middle section of the door came out crooked. Also, the left edge of the door was drawn a little too long. I have corrected these mistakes later.

Draw the sketch using light pencil strokes first, and then trace over them once you are satisfied with the proportions.

Start shading the darkest areas using brush pens/fat-tipped technical pens.

Notice that the front part of the church is in shadow, while the sun is brightly shining on the church diagonally from the right-hand side over its roof. That's why the front side of the hedge on the right-hand side is made extra dark.

Thicken the right-hand side edges of the crosses on the top. This will add some depth to them.

Add stonework to the church walls. Draw broken lines. We want the viewer's attention to the structure of the church. If we make the stonework too prominent, the picture will look too crowded. So, keep it subtle.

Also, note that the stonework is left unfinished on the right-hand side wall. The horizontal lines running along the planks over the roof are also left unfinished.

This is done deliberately to indicate the bright light falling on the slanting roof and the lower part of the right-hand wall. Brighter the light, then the less visible are the details.

Add some shading to the front parts of the church as shown below. If you want to push these surfaces toward darker shadows, you may want to consider cross-hatching.

Also, add some shadow to the wooden door of the church. I took the opportunity to correct the crooked middle line of the door while doing this.

You may remember my statement in 'The Fear of Making Mistakes' part at the beginning of the book. I said that correcting mistakes in a pen illustration is *not impossible*.

Well, here's your proof!

The Omnibus of Pen Sketching

Now shade the entire front part of the church. I chose to use hatching strokes to do this. Note that these hatching strokes are a little lighter than the hatching strokes used for the slanting roofs.

We do want consistency in shading different parts of the church. But we also want the viewer to visually differentiate between different parts of the building.

Add shadow to the right-hand side wall. This shadow should extend only to the edge of the stonework drawn over this wall.

The lower part of the wall (where no stonework was drawn) should be left alone from shading. This will automatically make it appear bright.

You may notice that I have also covered up the mistake in the left-hand side frame of the door. I have covered the mistake using the shadow over the pathway from the church door to the fence.

Partially add shadows to the slanting roof in the front. Since the light is falling on the church from the right-hand side, it will fall brightly on this slanting roof. But at the same time, it will be partially blocked by the bell tower on the right-hand side. The bell tower will cast its shadow over the slanting roof.

To make sure you remain within the confines set for this shadow, draw the shadow outline very lightly using a pencil. Then draw the hatching/cross-hatching lines keeping within this pencil line.

I decided to create a backdrop of trees for this church to draw even more attention to the main structure. This is totally optional, and you may skip this if you want. This is completely an artistic choice I made at that moment.

For illustrating the trees, I have drawn some branches and stems as shown behind the church.

I decided to draw these trees behind the church as silhouettes. The contrast of very dark tree outlines 'pops out' the church building even more.

After waiting for an hour, I added some random scribbles over the board on the right-hand side of the door using a white pen. I also used the white pen to tighten up some areas in the illustration.

Why wait for an hour? Because my experience is that a white pen does not work effectively over the black pen and brush pen marks when they are fresh. Even though this is a dry medium, the ink is not completely 'dry' for

another hour or so. After that, the white pen works like a charm!

After almost completing the illustration, I realized that I hadn't added any shadows to the fence. Since the light is falling from the right-hand side of the church, it's effectively behind the fence. So the shadow of the fence should fall over the pavement in the front. The same applies to the hedge.

The Omnibus of Pen Sketching

Complex Exercises

An Old Stone Building Converted into an Office

Let's draw this beautiful stone building in two-point perspective. This illustration is drawn using a reference photograph from Mount Airy, NC, USA shared with me by a FB friend, Emi.

We will use this reference photograph to do the illustration shown above.

You may download and use the reference photograph and the rough sketch from this web page:

https://HuesAndTones.net/slabreferences/

We will start with basic measurements of the building to find out the scope of our illustration.

I have used the approximate measurements of various sides of the building. These are not to-scale measurements, because our aim is to draw an expressive illustration.

Draw a sketch like this using the rough sketch provided. Use very light pencil strokes using an HB pencil.

P.S. Before drawing the illustration, check the Perspective section in Part 1 of this book to get the basics of two-point perspective correct.

To assist you in this illustration, I have added a couple of diagrams below, which will help you draw the correct perspective lines.

The vanishing points in the case of both the surfaces are way outside the paper. But you can still get the perspective lines right by tracing them over the edges of the surfaces as shown in the following two pictures.

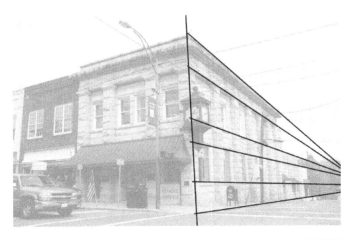

Once the pencil illustration is done, and you are satisfied that it has approximately correct proportions and perspective, let's start drawing light pen lines for foreground objects.

I almost always start with broken lines. This helps in correcting any early mistakes easily.

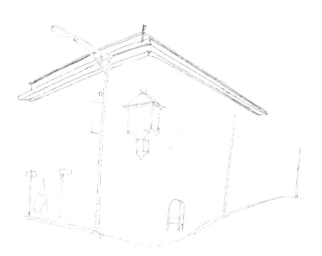

Start drawing the upper edges of the building. Notice that the lines for these edges are parallel to each other. But due to the perspective from which we are looking at the building, these edges appear to converge as they move away from us.

Add some details to the foreground objects like the electrical pole and the big wall clock.

Now let's start with the details of the wall on the left-hand side. Start drawing the horizontal lines for the doors and windows on this wall.

Just like the lines at the top of the building, these horizontal lines will converge in alignment with the perspective lines.

The Omnibus of Pen Sketching

Now draw the vertical lines joining these horizontal lines. The vertical lines will not converge like the horizontal lines. They will always be perpendicular to the ground level.

But as these vertical lines move away from the viewer, they will become smaller and smaller.

Start drawing the stripes over the awning. These stripes are parallel to each other over the curved surface of the awning.

While drawing such patterns over the awning like the one over the main door of this building, the danger is to get carried away and realize much later that we have missed the symmetry of the pattern. Like this.

To avoid this, I always draw the lines at various intervals first. Then close these intervals with more lines as shown below.

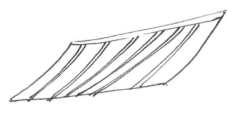

Let's do the same for the awnings of this building.

Mark the darkest areas using thick-tipped technical pens/brush pens. Observe that the lower edges of the windows on the upper floor are made dark as well. This creates a sense of depth for those windows.

Draw the stone patterns over the wall as shown below. I have used very thin strokes to indicate the stonework. If we draw thick lines for the stones, the viewer's attention may get diverted from the structure of the building to the stonework, which we don't want.

Start adding some texture to the stones of the top parapet. Notice the direction of the hatching lines. This direction helps in visually separating the horizontal and vertical surfaces.

I decided to completely darken the lower side of this parapet. It's your choice whether you want to do so.

Start shading the front part of the building. Two things to note here:
• The hatching lines are drawn in different directions as per the direction of the surface. Due to such diversity of hatching lines, it's easier for the viewer to visually differentiate the surfaces.
• The light and shadow areas were marked with pencils beforehand so that the pen strokes can be controlled while shading.

Add very light texture and shading to the front stone wall. Add hatching lines to shade the top of the window frames.

Add some shade to the glass panes of the windows. Keep some white space over the glass panes to indicate the reflections.

Complex Exercises

Add some shading and texture to the tapering right-hand side part of the parapet.

Start drawing the right-hand side of the building. Start with the broken lines as shown here.

We will not focus much on the details of the building on the right-hand side. This side is brightly lit, and thus the texture details will be less visible. Only the dark areas should be drawn in detail.

Add the finishing touches. Use light shading on the pillars. Reduce the details for the distant buildings.

Draw some overhanging wires. Drawing such wires gives a dynamic and interesting touch to the illustrations.

A Small Temple at the Crossroads

Let's draw this complex street scene.

I have done this illustration from a photograph from the old area of my city..

You may download and use the reference photograph and the rough sketch from this web page:

https://HuesAndTones.net/slabreferences/

Let's use the reference image below to draw this landscape. As you can see, it looks quite complex.

But worry not! We will learn to break this complex picture down into manageable chunks and then draw it.

Remember the magic mantra... Always divide and conquer!

The focal point of this picture is the small temple and the tree in the background. So, we will focus on these and put everything else in the background.

But I can see many human figures in that picture… you may say.

And you would be right. There are indeed many human figures in this photograph.

But is it necessary to draw human figures?

The simple answer is, No.

The artistic answer is, It depends!

But before you go ahead and skip this part entirely, listen to me.

Illustrating some human figures in the landscape is not absolutely necessary, but if drawn correctly, these human figures invoke a sense of scale (and soul) to the picture.

And surprisingly, it's not as hard as it seems!

For tips on easily drawing the human figures in a landscape, refer to the section 'Human Figures' in Part 1 of this book.

Let's get cracking.

Let's begin by drawing this rough sketch. You may add/remove any details as per your wish. Remember, an illustration is our *interpretation* of the scenery, not an exact copy. If we wanted to capture everything in a scene, we have separate devices to do that. They are called cameras!

These perspective lines will help us understand the angles of the rooftops and windows of the row of buildings on the right-hand side.

Observe that these lines are converging towards the left-hand side. They will eventually meet at a point (vanishing point) far outside the paper. You don't need to worry about it too much at this stage. Just lightly draw a bunch of such lines and keep the lines of the doors, windows, and rooftops aligned with these perspective lines.

Let's draw some human figures and this foreground pole.

Start drawing the temple. Start with the roof and the left-hand wall which is being overlapped by the pole and people. I have decided to draw only the outline for the building on the extreme left. Our focus will entirely be on the middle part of the illustration. The detailing will reduce as we go towards the edges.

Draw the fence of the temple and the right-hand side wall. Draw the outline of the big sign on the right-hand side behind the big umbrella.

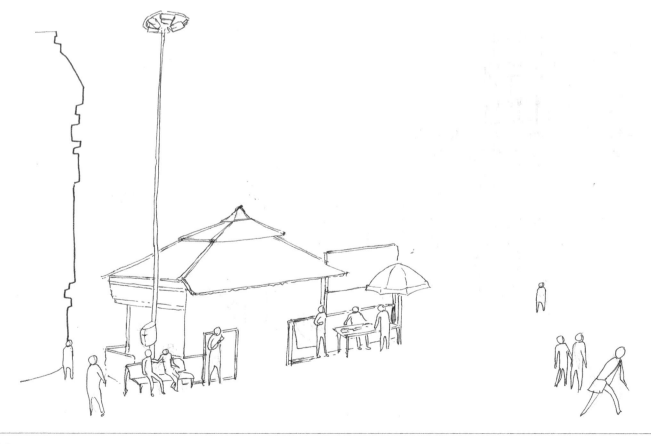

The Omnibus of Pen Sketching

Draw some details of the temple as shown below..

I have zoomed in to show you the details of the roof pattern and steps.

Start drawing the houses on the right-hand side. Keep the horizontal lines of those rooftops, doors, and windows aligned with the perspective lines. Draw the outlines for these houses using thin-tipped pens to make sure they are not as bold as those used for the temple.

Start drawing the foliage over the tree with scribble strokes. Since the tree foliage will overlap the background buildings on the right-hand side, we will hold off detailing those buildings until the tree is done.

Add some details to the tree using scribbling (random) strokes. When illustrating a tree this way, always make sure that you leave some gaps in the foliage. These gaps are called 'sky holes' and they are necessary to make the foliage look more natural.

When we are sure the tree details are complete, draw the remaining lines of the buildings on the right-hand side. Do not forget to continue these lines where they are visible through the sky holes.

The Omnibus of Pen Sketching

Shade the darkest areas using a brush pen, or a thick-tipped technical pen.

Observe that the notice board behind the umbrella is made completely dark. We will draw some letters on it using a white pen later. However, had we intended to color this illustration later, we would not have done so.

Start adding details to the right-hand side buildings. Use the slanting lines as shown to indicate the corrugated iron roofs.

We want to keep the details of these houses to a minimum. The vertical lines drawn over the walls serve the sole purpose of indicating a surface. If we keep the wall surfaces completely devoid of texture lines, they will look like blank spaces.

Let's draw the distant buildings on the right-hand side. These buildings should have even less detailing than the buildings we drew earlier. We use hatching strokes to draw only the shadows for these buildings. Use the thinnest tip pens for drawing these.

The same principle applies for the distant foliage on the left-hand side. Do not use hatching strokes over the entire area of the foliage. Keep some white space. This will create an illusion of various levels of foliage in the viewer's mind.

Apply dark shades to the inner walls of the temple. Use hatching strokes to shade the outer wall. Keep the shading on the outer wall lighter than that of the inner walls.

Shade the right-hand side of the post box over the pole to add some depth to it.

Draw some details over the umbrella and lightly shade a part of it.

The Omnibus of Pen Sketching

Lightly add some shadows on the left side of the building which is partially covered by the tree. Use hatching strokes to minimize its details.

Add some shadows to the people. Make sure that all the shadows are pointing in the same direction.

A shadow should always 'stick' to the foot of the subject. If a gap is left between a shadow and the person it belongs to, it will appear as if that person is floating in the air!

Drawing the shadows like this helps the viewer mentally place the various objects within the scene.

Complex Exercises

Add shading to the temple roof. Add a horizontal line extending from the middle of the left-hand wall of the temple till the left-most building. This is our horizon line. All the background foliage behind the temple on the left-hand side should be above this horizon line.

I have also chosen to add some overhanging wires. Although these wires look very ugly in real life, they add a different charm and dynamism to an illustration. So, I suggest to always use them to your advantage.

Even though we are using a dry medium like pens, the pen marks may not respond like a dry surface when you use a white pen to add finishing touches. I always wait an hour or two after my illustration is done before I use a white pen over the black pen/brush pen marks.

I have also used the white pen to add some random letters to the board partially overlapped by the umbrella.

A House in Hawaii

Let's draw this beautiful scenery with the house. This illustration is done from a reference photograph shared by my FB friend Emi.

Notice the following points in this landscape:

• The three house buildings and the nearby shade with solar panels are the focal points and will be drawn with the maximum clarity.
• The fence in the foreground is deliberately left without any details. We could have drawn textures and shades over the wood. But it would take the focus away from the main elements. We don't want that. Of course, this is my choice. If you feel that the fence should be shown with a texture, you are free to do so.

• The distant elements like the mountains are drawn in much less detail to 'push' them to the background.

You may download and use the reference photograph and the rough sketch from this web page:

https://HuesAndTones.net/slabreferences/

We will use these two photographs in combination since none of them are enough to draw the complete details.

You may notice that the main house building is partially covered by a big hedge in the foreground. We will not include this hedge in our illustration.

This is the initial illustration. The distant elements are very lightly marked with dotted lines. We will keep the details of them to a minimum.

Start with the roof of the main building. The roof shingles should be drawn with a thin-tipped pen. I have drawn them with broken lines.

We want to draw the viewer's attention towards the main structure of the building.

Also, the roof is bathed under bright light. So, we will keep the details to a minimum.

Draw the chimney over the roof of the main house. Use random strokes to indicate the stone structure of the chimney. Draw the outline of the adjoining building.

Draw the details of the windows and doors of the three foreground buildings as shown.

Draw the fence outline. We will not add any details here.

Start with the darkest areas of the hedges. I have used a brush pen to darken these areas. You may use a brush pen or a fat-tipped technical pen to do this.

Draw the roof of the second building using cross-hatching.

The Omnibus of Pen Sketching

Add some details to the hedges and trees in the foreground and the middle ground.

Draw some brickwork over the first two buildings. Draw some deep shadows below these buildings as shown.

Shade the front part of the first three buildings using hatching strokes. Complete the shadows of the buildings by extending the originally drawn deep shadows with hatching strokes.

Draw the partial shadow on the right-hand side of the first building. Since light is falling on this building from the right-hand side, the bottom part of the right-side wall of the first building will be brightly lit. The upper part will have a shadow cast on it from the slanting roof.

Draw the shadow over the fourth building (the one with the solar panels). The left-hand side of this building will be completely covered in shadow since it's facing away from the light. The front side of this building will have a diagonally cast shadow from its front roof.

Draw the roof of the building across the road and the hedges near that building.

Shade the pole behind the main building.

The Omnibus of Pen Sketching

Add very dark shadow on the left-hand side of the solar panel building. Start drawing the tree behind the first building.

Mark a very dark area for the very distant house. This dark area will be on the left-hand side of the distant house.

Completely darken the compound wall behind the solar panels. Add details to the tree behind the first building.

Start illustrating the foliage behind the three main buildings using stippling.

Draw the background trees and foliage. We will keep them very light. We want to push this part of the landscape to the background.

The Omnibus of Pen Sketching

As we go away from the main buildings of focus, the detailing should become less and less. This will create an illusion of depth in the landscape.

In the remaining steps, we will use this same principle to draw distant elements like trees, foliage, and mountains with diminishing details.

n the end, we will add some finishing touches by making sure that correct shadows are drawn for each element and adding some blades of grass in the foreground area surrounding the main three buildings.

ABOUT THE AUTHOR

Shirish is a self-taught artist based in a very populous city called Pune, in a very populous country called India.

Shirish has worked in the thriving IT Industry for more than two decades. But he is an artist at heart. Drawing, painting and teaching art is his first, second and third love (not necessarily in that sequence!).

Shirish dabbles in various subjects such as landscapes, portraits, figure studies, and abstracts. He works in various media like pen & ink, watercolor, oil, acrylic, digital and spray paint.

Shirish has participated in many art exhibitions. His illustrations and paintings are present in private collections in India and various other countries.

Shirish has published some very successful video courses, which he produces himself. These courses have been viewed and admired by thousands of students worldwide.

Shirish is the author of various bestselling art instruction books.

Social Media

If you want regular updates and free goodies from me, consider subscribing to my mailing list. I never share your email ID with anyone because I hate spam as much as you do.

But I do believe in sharing a lot of quality content with my readers and offering them discounts. When you subscribe to my mailing list, you will get a printable PDF of my adult colouring book 'Dystopian Encounters' as well as some more free goodies.

You can get access of a host of free training materials and videos on my website. You can also check out my other books (available in multiple languages) on my website. All of my social media links are also given on the next few pages.

https://HuesAndTones.net/signup/

The Omnibus of Pen Sketching

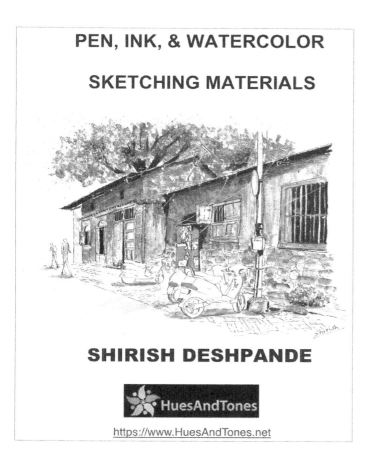

PEN, INK, & WATERCOLOR

SKETCHING MATERIALS

SHIRISH DESHPANDE

HuesAndTones
https://www.HuesAndTones.net

DYSTOPIAN ENCOUNTERS – WAVE 1

MUSINGS FROM ANOTHER DIMENSION
– AN ADULT COLORING BOOK

Illustrated by:
Shirish Deshpande

Email: shirishauthor@gmail.com

Website: https://HuesAndTones.net/

Books:
https://HuesAndTones.net/books/

Video Trainings:
https://HuesAndTones.net/courses/

YouTube:
https://Youtube.com/c/huesandtones/

Art Gallery:
https://www.behance.net/shirishd

The Omnibus of Pen Sketching

Facebook:
https://www.facebook.com/HuesAndTones-135547303183050

Instagram: HuesAndTones1 (note the '1' at the end)
https://www.instagram.com/huesandtones1/

Pinterest: HuesAndTones
https://in.pinterest.com/sd2313/

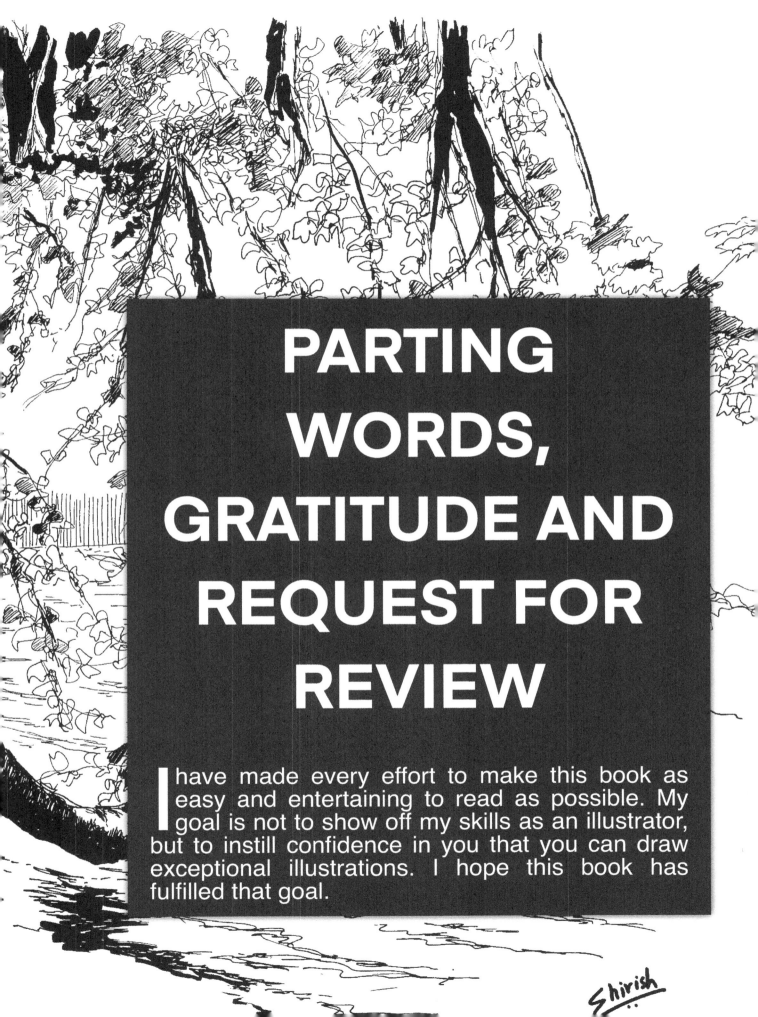

PARTING WORDS, GRATITUDE AND REQUEST FOR REVIEW

I have made every effort to make this book as easy and entertaining to read as possible. My goal is not to show off my skills as an illustrator, but to instill confidence in you that you can draw exceptional illustrations. I hope this book has fulfilled that goal.

Shirish

I am sure this book dissipated your fear of pen and ink drawing (if you had one).

I will repeat the same nugget of wisdom that I have mentioned so many times before.

Do not be afraid to experiment.

Happy sketching :-)

Gratitude

I am extremely grateful to my wife Aparna. She has consistently stood with me, encouraged me and tolerated me through all my artistic endeavors and eccentricities.

Thank you Emi (@emi_sisk on Instagram) for sharing some of the most amazing images of your town. Several of these images were used as references for the illustrations in this book.

I am thankful to the many fellow artists, authors, and creatives, who keep inspiring me every day. You guys are awesome!

Did you receive any value from this book? Did you enjoy reading it?

If yes, would you please leave a review on the store from where you bought this book?

Your review will help the book reach more readers worldwide and help them learn to sketch like a boss.

After all, the joy multiplies when shared, right? :-)

Made in the USA
Monee, IL
28 May 2022